"No one is better qualified to lead a conversation neuroscience than Malcolm Jeeves. As lecturer, author and practitioner, he has been central to the discussion for decades, and he brings to this book uncommon wisdom, practical insight and a rare combination of expertise and humility. For anyone interested in what recent innovations in brain science might contribute to our understanding of what it means to be human, this is a must-read."

Joel B. Green, *Fuller Theological Seminary, author of* Bodies, Souls, and Human Life: The Nature of Humanity in the Bible

"What is the relationship between the brain and the mind? What about the soul: Does it exist? Is it something other than just the brain or brain activity? Do we have a God gene? If you want to explore possible answers to these and very many other related questions, you will want to read *Minds, Brains, Souls and Gods.* It offers much to learn and much to ponder. Malcolm Jeeves is a distinguished neurobiologist, at home also with the Bible and Christian and other religious traditions. Jeeves's conversational style is highly didactic, as well as entertaining. A pleasure to read."

Francisco J. Ayala, *Donald Bren Professor of Biological Sciences at the University of California, Irvine*

"This is a bold, timely, remarkable and impressive book. No one should doubt its colossal and up-to-date learning in psychology, neuroscience, evolutionary theory and cognate fields. What makes it especially remarkable is the combination of all this with a sober, realistic and accurate understanding of many biblical passages and theological doctrines. The book engages with many issues that impinge on Christian faith: the existence of the 'soul,' determinism and freedom, altruism, divine guidance, reductionism, evolutionary theory, genetics and a host of such issues. The style, on top of all this, is extremely readable, and is modeled on the dialogical correspondence of C. S. Lewis's *Screwtape Letters* and *Letters to Malcolm.* However, these are genuine questions, not hypothetical ones, based largely on real questions raised by Christian psychology students at Hope College (Holland, Michigan) and elsewhere. The upshot is that in the search for truth, Prof. Jeeves argues, there is no conflict between psychology or neuroscience and Christian belief or theology. These are not competitors but complementary ways of approaching truth. This book avoids any bland generalization and patiently explores each source of concern as raised by students. It conveys the careful Christian thought of a dedicated academic career of well over half a century. It has extensive bibliographies. I have no hesitation in warmly and unreservedly commending this marvelous book."

Canon Anthony C. Thiselton, *University of Nottingham*

"This remarkably accessible volume brings a lifetime of scientific engagement at the highest level to bear on the kinds of questions posed by contemporary science in general, and psychology, neuroscience and evolutionary biology in particular. Although it focuses specifically on those questions raised at the cutting edge of contemporary psychology, its range extends well beyond the bounds of that discipline. As Jeeves comments in the preface, the questions it addresses are 'real questions raised by real students who want to be intellectually honest, to have . . . examined faith.' What results from this honest and informed engagement is the recognition that, far from being in tension with the deliverances of science, Christian faith opens and liberates the mind to grasp the truth at ever-deeper levels. Jeeves avoids the confused assumption that Christians have to pinpoint an essential distinguishing factor between the human being and other creatures, since 'as Christians we believe that . . . what makes us different is not something about us but who we are called to be.' The perception underpinning the book is that God addresses and calls precisely those same creatures upon which evolutionary biology, neuroscience and the rest of the scientific disciplines stand to shed so much light.

While this volume is remarkably wide-ranging in the questions it asks, it also engages in profound and deep-thinking (yet always lucid) analysis. For those cynics who would dismiss Christianity with uninformed or superficial references to the scientific state of play, this volume is bad news. For those Christians, of any age, who fear lest their faith may require them to put intellectual rigor or scientific integrity to one side, it is exceedingly good news. This is a superb book which I vehemently hope—and, indeed, fully expect—will become a best-seller. Every Christian student interested in the fundamental questions of human nature and scientific inquiry must buy it, read it and pass it on to their friends!"

Alan J. Torrance, *St. Mary's College, University of St Andrews*

Minds, Brains, Souls and Gods

A Conversation on Faith, Psychology and Neuroscience

Malcolm Jeeves

An imprint of InterVarsity Press
Downers Grove, Illinois

InterVarsity Press
P.O. Box 1400, Downers Grove, IL 60515-1426
World Wide Web: www.ivpress.com
Email: email@ivpress.com

InterVarsity Press® is the book-publishing division of InterVarsity Christian Fellowship/USA®, a movement of students and faculty active on campus at hundreds of universities, colleges and schools of nursing in the United States of America, and a member movement of the International Fellowship of Evangelical Students. For information about local and regional activities, write Public Relations Dept., InterVarsity Christian Fellowship/USA, 6400 Schroeder Rd., P.O. Box 7895, Madison, WI 53707-7895, or visit the IVCF website at www.intervarsity.org.

Cover design: Cindy Kiple
Interior design: Beth Hagenberg
Images: Tim Teebken/Getty Images

ISBN 978-0-8308-3998-8 (print)
ISBN 978-0-8308-9562-5 (digital)

Printed in the United States of America ∞

InterVarsity Press is committed to protecting the environment and to the responsible use of natural resources. As a member of Green Press Initiative we use recycled paper whenever possible. To learn more about the Green Press Initiative, visit www.greenpressinitiative.org.

Library of Congress Cataloging-in-Publication Data

Davis, Dale Ralph.
The message of Daniel : His kingdom cannot fail / Dale Ralph Davis.
pages cm.—(The Bible speaks today series)
Includes bibliographical references.
ISBN 978-0-8308-2438-0 (pbk. : alk. paper)
1. Bible. Daniel—Commentaries. I. Title.
BS1555.53.D38 2013
224'.507—dc23

2013015292

P 21 20 19 18 17 16 15 14 13 12 11 10 9 8 7 6 5 4 3 2 1
Y 31 30 29 28 27 26 25 24 23 22 21 20 19 18 17 16 15 14 13

For

Sarah and Joanna

Contents

Preface

Robert Boyle, illustrious scientist and Fellow of the Royal Society, described how, while in Geneva on a continental holiday, he underwent a conversion from nominal, unthinking Christianity to committed Christianity. As a result of his experiences, he stressed the need for Christians to have what he called an "examined faith."[1]

John Stott, discussing Paul's letter to the Christians at Philippi, drew attention to the importance for all Christians to heed the apostle's exhortation to "contend for the faith of the Gospel." He continues, "This describes a combination of evangelism and apologetics, not only proclaiming the gospel, but also defending it and arguing for its truth."[2]

Echoing the views of Robert Boyle and John Stott, Mark Noll says, "If what we claim about Jesus Christ is true, then evangelicals should be among the most active, most serious, and most open-minded advocates of general human learning."[3]

The New Testament accounts of the spread of the Christian gospel—the good news of God's redeeming love in Jesus Christ—vividly illustrate how the gospel both warms the heart and engages the mind. These are not mutually exclusive but reciprocally reinforcing. As the love of God in Christ warms the heart and engages the emotions, it generates a desire to know more; as the mind is engaged in the voyage of discovery, the things learned warm the heart even more, and on it goes. Research findings in psychology and related subjects such as neuroscience produce fresh challenges for our generation to develop an "examined faith," engaging both heart and mind.

It appears that university students are responding to such challenges. Admissions to psychology courses in colleges and universities have risen steadily for half a century, a trend that shows no signs of diminishing.

Course contents vary enormously; nevertheless, students seeking a degree in psychology normally cover certain core topics.

There are international differences in the faith commitments of students taking core psychology courses. A recent survey of more than 100,000 freshmen in California showed that 80 percent of college freshmen believe in God, 70 percent of them admit to grappling with big questions about the meaning of life, and more than two-thirds pray. This general picture was endorsed by the latest data from *The American Freshman,* an annual UCLA survey of a quarter of a million students entering all sorts of American colleges and universities.[4] It showed that all but 22 percent claim some sort of religious affiliation. I am not aware of any recent comparable figures for the United Kingdom, but surveys of the general population suggest that a very small percentage of the students enrolling in psychology courses would admit to believing in God or being religious.

A Christian student taking a psychology course in Britain may find herself a lonely figure. The beliefs she brings from her local church seem, at times, to conflict with the pronouncements of her lecturers, especially on topics such as evolutionary psychology and neuropsychology. The typical psychology student in America—more so than in the UK—will likely have the benefit of friendship with fellow Christians, but the evidence shows that the majority of even American students grapple with issues that arise as their religious beliefs seem to conflict with what they are taught in their psychology lectures.

Listen to this cri de coeur that a friend of mine received from a psychology major at a leading US university. It alone would justify the writing of this book. The student wrote:

> Hello! . . . I took AP Psychology for a semester in high school using your psychology textbook. . . . I am a very devout Christian, although still exploring the specifics of what I believe as a Christian. . . . I am taking a Psychology 100 course, and after only one day I feel a bit weighed down religiously. I don't think my professor is a Christian (What a shock! Haha.), and the book talks, of course, about how everything we do is based on genetics or experience, and we don't have free will, since all of our thoughts and actions are basically one huge reflex—a long chain of events of experiences and associations reacting with our genes, etc.

> I just feel a bit strange, like there is a big knot in my throat or in my heart when I read the book. The idea that everything about us is either based on genetics or experience seems to clash with the idea of free will, and makes me question who exactly I "am" at all, if I am just a combination of coincidences, and yet, what bothers me really is that it seems perfectly correct—I can't think of an alternative to that idea of "nature vs. nurture = me." The book also talks about how we don't have souls (implies it at least), because we are directly connected to our physical bodies (our brains). That could be well and true—I'm not actually sure if I believe in a literal soul, at least a soul separate from the body, but I think I believe there should be something about us that is more than just organs, something made in the image of God, something different from animals that has the potential to exist eternally (although, the Bible does say we will be given new bodies or something like that . . . although that fixes part of my dilemma, wouldn't the fact that the bodies are "new" make us different people, since we are what our bodies make us?).
>
> The class is going to be a challenge for me, and I not only want to come out feeling just as strong or stronger in my faith, but I want to be able to defend my faith if the situation should arise—especially if there are any other wondering Christians in my class.
>
> So, I'm not exactly sure what I am asking, but you are the first person I thought of. I was just wondering if you or your coworkers had any thoughts, ideas, advice or information that could help me in my thoughts and help me through my psychology class, since I'm sure you've thought about ideas along these lines a lot throughout your studies and teaching. . . . I'd really appreciate anything small to put my foot on.

No student has time for everything. All feel under pressure. Even if they were inclined to consult the ever-increasing number of high-powered tomes discussing challenges to traditional Christian beliefs from developments in science, there just is not time. Typically such volumes bring together leading scientists, philosophers, theologians and biblical scholars. Whilst they make significant contributions to ongoing debates, being written by specialists for specialists, they are, at times, difficult reading for interested amateurs.

Having been privileged to participate in some of these meetings, I have at times come away feeling what a shame it is that some of the very helpful and wise words I have listened to could not be shared more widely.[5] Some of the meetings resulted in books, but even in those, discussions were often at a level not easily accessible to nonspecialists in the fields. I have done my best in what follows to share some of these insights and comments with a typical college student launching out into the field of psychology.

A Christian joining a local IVCF chapter in the U.S., or Christian Union (UCCF) group in Britain, finds himself a member of a group aiming to share their faith with other students. Personal evangelism is encouraged, as it was fifty years ago when an article appeared—first in *Inter Varsity,* the student magazine of British UCCF, and then reprinted in *HIS* magazine, the student publication of IVCF in America—that painted a scenario of student evangelism in action. Its message is still relevant. Consider these excerpts (making due allowance for something written fifty years ago):

> Come with me, if you will, to the student union of any college, and listen to an Inter-Varsity fellow talking over a coke to another student. He has (with some difficulty and some prayer) brought the conversation around to "spiritual things" and is now following his usual pattern for getting down to the gospel.
>
> All goes well until he finds that his non-Christian friend has intellectual difficulties on matters about which he has never really thought. He therefore finds it hard to believe that they are genuine. And since he can't answer them anyway, he assumes that they are only a smokescreen for moral difficulties. His friend is only putting them up to avoid getting down to the "real issues." . . . A period of verbal fencing follows. . . . His friend just doesn't want to face up to the message of the Gospel. After all, what other reason could there be? The Christian student feels that he has demonstrated clearly how simply his friend's questions can be answered. And besides, the point doesn't seem to him either interesting or important. It is obviously a "red herring."

The article ends,

> It is all too easy to assume that every herring is a "red herring." I want to suggest, then, that intellectual difficulties need not be irksome hindrances interfering with our personal work but rather doors which may open to life eternal. Willingness to think with our friends through these problems will become an evidence of our friendship and a way of gaining confidence in each other's sincerity of purpose and honesty of mind. Contacts made in this way can be as productive of close and profitable friendships as those made on athletic teams or in the laboratory.[6]

Today, more than half a century later, there is an increasing recognition among Christians, in the words of the widely read book *Moving Toward Emmaus* by David Smith, that "embedded at the very centre of the Christian story is the principle that genuine faith cannot be compelled. . . . When Christianity became the dominant religion in Europe, attaining both social prestige and political power, it quickly forgot the example of its Founder and invented a whole battery of methods to coerce people into allegiance to this religion, and then to ensure that they never abandoned it."[7]

Today, Smith argues, we must revisit the Christ of the Emmaus road, who depicted God himself in a revolutionary manner as "the waiting Father" (Luke 15:11-32). We have the privilege to walk alongside fellow puzzled inquirers, remembering, as Smith says, that "with all the props and social supports of Christendom removed, believers realized that the gospel itself contained an imperative demanding the rejection once and for all of 'the *obligatory, compulsory God* whom believers impose on their fellow human beings, over-riding their minds and consciences and even threatening sanctions in the case of non-conformity.'"[8]

My contacts over half a century with students taking psychology courses have alerted me to the actual problems they confront. That was one reason why, more than fifty years ago, I wrote the *HIS Magazine* article quoted above. I have checked my own impressions through invaluable feedback from two professors of psychology at Hope College in the U.S., David Myers and Thomas Ludwig, who recently ran a semester-long course on psychology and religion. They kindly kept a record of the actual questions raised by the students throughout the course. As I put these together with the questions of which I was already aware through my personal contact with students, certain recurring core issues emerged. In this small book I have engaged in dialogue with an imaginary student as he progresses through his four-year honors course in psychology and faces these core questions.

Problems and questions do not end with graduation. An engineering postgraduate student in a Far East country recently wrote to a Christian faculty friend of mine in North America, asking for help after reading one of my friend's books. He wrote, "Faith is something I desperately want, but find it hard to reconcile with the realities of science and of the world around me." His emails to my friend led to a series of exchanges during which my friend shared with him some of the early draft sections of this little book, which addresses some of the issues he raised. He found them helpful. I hope you, the reader, will also. People of all academic backgrounds and careers struggle with contemporary challenges to their faith. This month I read of a Christian professor of physics in a South American country who wrote, "I think one of the greatest challenges is to integrate my faith into my academic work. . . . This challenge requires reflection and it helps to know how people in other places in a similar situation have overcome it."[9] I hope my experience, as it emerges from these pages, will help him and others like him.

The topics covered are not necessarily the ones that the high-powered academics I referred to earlier may have written about, although there is doubtless some overlap. These are *real questions* raised by *real students* who want to be intellectually honest, to have Robert Boyle's *examined faith* and who want, as John Stott suggests, "a combination of evangelism and apologetics, not only proclaiming the gospel, but also defending it and arguing for its truth."[10] We need Christians ready to walk along the Emmaus road in the company of the risen Christ with fellow disciples who are, at times, puzzled.

We all have questions and puzzles about aspects of our faith, and we can find mutual support and encouragement as we honestly share them. We need this supportive sharing, because, as Tom Wright has reminded us, "There is a persistent untruth which has made its way into the popular imagination in our day: that Christianity means closing off your mind, ceasing all serious thought, and living in a shallow fantasy world divorced from the solid truths of 'real life.'" "But," he continues, "the truth is that genuine Christianity opens the mind [as Paul has been saying throughout this letter (to the Ephesians), and in its companion piece, the letter to Colossae], so that it can grasp truth at deeper and deeper levels."[11]

Almost half a century ago, C. S. Lewis wrote his *Letters to Malcolm: Chiefly on Prayer*.[12] I found them, then and now, helpful and heartwarming. With those letters in mind, and being daily in touch with colleagues, students and friends through email, I have used today's letter format in this little book.

As the email correspondence developed, the topics raised by students through my personal experience over many years and by those taught by David Myers and Thomas Ludwig began to fall naturally under a series of different themes. I have grouped the email exchanges under these themes and topics.

For any who do have the time and motivation to delve more deeply into some of the issues covered, I have provided in the endnotes, as well as the Further Reading section at the back of the book, references to up-to-date sources that will normally be available in college and university libraries or on the Web. This material gives the detailed evidence for some of the cryptic comments and assertions that typically occur in email exchanges.

1

What Is Psychology, and How Should We Approach It?

Ben,

Your father keeps me up to date with how you and your brothers are getting on in school. He tells me you have been accepted to the university of your choice. Congratulations. Your grades must have been good to succeed in such a competitive market. The psychology department has a high reputation. Each university psychology course has its own distinctive strengths, depending on the research interests of the staff. Yours is well-known for its scientific rigor and for majoring in areas of psychology that overlap with neuroscience and evolutionary biology. If the department has a short course on the history of psychology, I'd advise you to take it. It is so important to know how psychology arrived where it is today. It helps put current trends in perspective.

Malcolm,

Thanks! I'm excited to be here and wondering what I'm going to encounter in my psychology courses. To be honest, my parents aren't enthusiastic about my studying psychology. They think it could undermine my Christian faith. What reactions do you get from people, especially other Christians, to your being a psychology professor?

Ben,

The answer is, mixed reactions. Sadly, some Christians see psychology as an archenemy of the faith, a view perhaps reinforced by surveys of U.S. academics that show psychology faculty members to be the least religious group. Given the media treatment of some advances in psychology, I can understand your parents' concerns.

Ask ten friends what they think psychology is about, and you will probably get as many different answers. However, you may detect three major themes: first, that psychological knowledge is primarily to help people cope with mental and emotional problems; second, if they are avid magazine readers and TV watchers, that it is about the links between what is happening in our minds and brains; and third, with celebration of Darwin, that it is about how human psychological characteristics evolved from rudimentary forms elsewhere in the animal kingdom.

The first view is widely held in Christian circles. Half a century ago in North America, the Christian Association for Psychological Studies was established to provide a forum for discussions about psychology, counseling and Christian faith. Since then the majority of their activities and publications have focused on counseling and clinical psychology. The overwhelming majority of their members are affiliated with these specializations, which are evident in the Association's journal. All for good reasons. Their primary concern is to help others, fulfilled in the day-to-day, practical concerns of counselors, psychotherapists and clinical psychologists.

This helping theme continues a nineteenth-century approach in which almost all major Christian groups assumed a seamless relationship between "psychological care" and "soul care." In due course the meaning of "psychology" began to change, and its earlier limited scope became almost unrecognizable to a typical twenty-first-century psychology major.

Sadly, as psychology developed, its previous amicable relationship with religion began to change. First came the early-twentieth-century development of Freud's psychoanalysis. Then came the mid-century emergence—and, for a while, dominance—of behaviorism. Coincidentally, both of these specializations enjoyed high profiles in the nonscientific popular media. For example, psychoanalytic concepts and terms such as *Oedipus complex*, *repression* and *guilt complex* cropped up in literature, drama and everyday speech. Behaviorist terms also became widespread: people were *conditioned* to do this or *inhibited* from doing that.

The second and third themes, linking mind with brain and tracing out the evolutionary emergence of mind, find strong support if you look at a typical twenty-first-century college or university psychology textbook. There you find many references to the biological bases of cognition and behavior. For example, consider the ninth edition of David Myers's *Psychology*, the most widely used North American textbook of psychology. Of the sixteen chapters, three deal with personality, psychotherapy and social psychology; one addresses methodology; and the remaining twelve, making up 70 percent of the text, deal with psychological topics for which awareness of their neural and evolutionary roots is important. The balance is made up of other heavily biological topics such as emotion and stress.[1] So, while psychology is a professional practice in the clinics, in the universities it is a science.

Malcolm,

Thanks for the background information on the perception of psychology. I have only attended a couple of lectures so far, but I don't get the sense that people here embrace either Freud or Skinner. They seem to lean more toward the second and third themes you mentioned, linking mind with brain and tracing the evolution of human psychology.

Ben,

I'm not surprised. I think you will find that today most of your lecturers will be grateful inheritors of what has become known as the "cognitive revolution," which occurred as a reaction to the dominant behaviorist outlook in psychology at the middle of the last century. Howard Gardner, a psychology professor at Harvard, wrote a fascinating book on this so-called cognitive revolution. He recorded some of the recollections of Professor George Miller, a psychologist at MIT around the same time that the leading behaviorist, Professor Skinner, was at Harvard. Gardner recalls how George Miller went to a small international conference in Cambridge in the UK in 1956. Miller wrote, "I went away from the symposium with the strong conviction, more intuitive than rational, that human experimental psychology, theoretical linguistics and computer simulation of cognitive processes are all pieces of a larger whole, and that the future would see progressive elaboration and coordination of their shared concerns."[2]

An editorial in the journal *Science* in 1997, reflecting on fifty years of psychology, read, "The promise that Miller envisioned in those early days has come to pass." It went on, "The remarkable progress that has been made in recent years is beginning to generate excitement outside of the scientific community because of its relevance to our daily lives in shedding light on normal cognitive functions (such as language, memory, and planning) and on brain-related diseases (such as schizophrenia and Alzheimer's disease)."[3] I was at that Cambridge meeting in 1956 acting as its secretary. My role was to help my research supervisor, Sir Frederic Bartlett, organize the meeting. I fully agree with George Miller's account of what happened at that time. Many see that conference in Cambridge as the start of the cognitive revolution.

As I write this, I see that George Miller has just died at the age of ninety-two. On August 2, 2012, the *New York Times* noted that in 1955, psychological research was in a rut when a paper by George Miller "set off an explosion of new thinking about thinking and opened a new field of research known as cognitive psychology."[4]

Malcolm,
With all due respect, 1956 and 1997 seem like a long time ago to me. Where is the action today?

Ben,
The cognitive revolution continues and now has, in part, merged with developments in neuroscience. For example, just today I read a report underlining how an understanding of brain processes, combined with developments in cognitive psychology, is continuing to revolutionize our understanding of mental illnesses. This report comes from a laboratory in Cambridge and is titled "New Blood-Test to Aid in Schizophrenia Diagnosis." It quotes the lead researcher, Professor Sabine Bahn: "Schizophrenia is a complicated and challenging disease, yet current diagnostic approaches continue to be based on patient interviews and a subjective assessment of clinical symptoms. We expect [our new technique] to be used as an aid to this current process, and we hope it will provide the psychiatrist with additional confidence in their evaluation, as well as speed up the process."[5]

I have received another report from the Academy of Medical Sciences in Britain that draws attention to the rapid advance in research of dementia. It points out that by 2040 about 80 million people will be living with dementia—a very worrying statistic and a good reason why so much effort today is being put into studying this illness, trying to understand what is happening in the brain when it occurs.[6]

Another recent report explodes a myth that has been widely held until now. People once believed that the prevalence of dementia in developing countries was low. But now an international collaboration at the Institute of Psychiatry in London has shown that past estimates have substantially underestimated its prevalence in low- and middle-income countries, and it is almost as common as in developed countries. My point in sharing these examples is simple: what is widely accepted at one time can quickly be overturned by the emergence of new evidence.

Malcolm,

It sounds like you're pretty confident in the scientific approach to psychology. I'm still not quite sure. Even before I started school, I read enough to know that the views of Sigmund Freud, so dominant in the early twentieth century, are not taken very seriously by today's psychologists. Our textbook reflects that—Freud's views are only a handful of pages out of more than seven hundred. So while I agree that science has taught us a lot, I worry that we may put it on too high a pedestal. Even so, I am taking neuroscience as well as psychology because from my general reading I have seen how research in neuroscience is directly relevant to applications of psychology like clinical psychology, and that I am very interested in.

Ben,

I see your point. Regarding balance, I think that science, including the scientific approach to psychology, does have much to offer today's world. However, with great success in scientific work comes the temptation to develop a misunderstanding of the scientific enterprise. As the example of changing views about dementia shows, at times we have to realize that the assertions that come from science are tentative. This point was made very recently by the President of the Royal Society of London, Lord Martin Rees, in an article titled "Keeping It Real." Rees says, "Science isn't dogma: its assertions are sometimes tentative, sometimes compelling. The hardest situation to portray is where there is a strong consensus but some dissent. Controversy, confrontations and skepticism about Orthodoxy have such public appeal."[7] Current debates about the evidence for climate change are a good example of this.

Science is not something that stands alone from the rest of the world. As Martin Rees also says, "The applications and priorities of science should not be decided by scientists alone. There are political, economic and ethical dimensions." He argues that science matters to everyone: "You can appreciate the essence of science without being a scientist, in the same way you can appreciate music without being able to read a score or play an instrument."

I suspect that with so much media attention on developments in psychology, you in your generation will have an important part to play in doing your best to give a balanced, realistic, evidence-based account of what psychological research really is and is not producing.

Lord Rees's theme was also taken up by one of his recent predecessors as president of the Royal Society, Sir Michael Atiyah, one of the world's greatest living mathematicians. He commented, "There is a lot of public interest in science, and a real understanding of its benefits, but there is also a fear. This growing reaction against science—particularly its impact on the environment—has come about as the applications of science have had a greater impact on our lives. If you did all your science in the laboratory, then only a small number would care but, because we don't, more people are questioning its impact."[8]

When it comes to questions about how "scientific" psychology is or should aim to be, you will find a spectrum of views among Christians who have a shared faith perspective. You're not the only one who fears that the so-called scientific approach to psychology may, at times, lead to a failure to recognize the potential contribution that psychologists can make in fields that would not claim to be scientific. Psychotherapists have to deal with immediate pressing problems and so, understandably, protest that they do not have the luxury of waiting until the latest properly designed empirical investigation into a particular kind of therapy has been completed and published.

Psychologists are not the only ones who understand human nature. Shakespeare's plays are full of deep psychological insights into human nature. Sally Shuttleworth of Oxford University has reminded us that developmental psychology did not start with Jean Piaget but in literature. She cites how books by Dickens and the Brontes represented the child's mind from the inside and had a huge influence on child psychology and psychiatry. Shuttleworth believes that the actual start of child psychology can be traced to Charles Darwin's 1877 book *A Biographical Sketch of an Infant*.[9] Even some of the books of the Bible, such as Proverbs and Psalms, are full of profound insights into human nature.

I just received a book that describes five different approaches that Christians have taken to relating what is happening in psychology with what Christians have traditionally believed.[10] Some of the contributors support your concerns that an overly scientific approach misses important things that psychology can teach us. Other contributors feel strongly that psychology, and particularly modern psychology, has been in error by not making greater references to religion. The whole area of what is called "transformational psychology," for example, would see the scientific approach as too limited, a view shared by some of those psychologists who are engaged primarily in clinical psychology and counseling.

2

What Is the Relationship Between the Mind and the Brain?

Malcolm,

I'll admit that I do feel at least some fear when reading about studies that seem to reduce the mind, or some mental experiences, to the activity of a brain circuit.

Ben,

I understand your concerns. Nowhere is the questioning of science more necessary than when you read the dramatic reports of research on brain and mind. In December 2011, Professor John Stein, a leading Oxford neuroscientist, wrote, "Claims are being made about brain research that just aren't true, and they are being accepted uncritically by the press, the public, policy makers and even the courts."[1] He warned about the increasing dominance of reductionism. He noted that "scientists [are] picking off the relatively easy tasks of working out how little bits of the brain work molecularly and hoping that knowing about these nuts and bolts will eventually tell us how the complex system works as a whole." He adds, "However, there are no complex systems whose emergent properties can be deduced from the molecular structure alone. . . . Even in physics the flow of explanation is usually in the other direction: theoreticians develop models of the system and use these to predict the properties of individual elements. But such systems thinkers are becoming increasingly rare in neuroscience." Professor Stein commends the work of the Brain Mind Forum, which aims to get neuroscientists to "think about why they are doing what they are doing, and have the courage to ask questions that are currently forbidden, like what is consciousness, and what is the relationship between mind and brain."[2]

The problem, however, is that headlines claim that we have identified the cause of depression or love or autism or Alzheimer's, just because an area of the brain lights up in association with each of those. But correlations are not causes. Finding causes is often very difficult.

Malcolm,

Part of what triggered my own interest in psychology was reading news reports about how the brain makes the mind. I find it intriguing. As I said before, though, it's a bit scary. I wonder what studying psychology is going to do to my own self-understanding.

Ben,

Public interest in psychological research is perfectly understandable. There have been some remarkable advances in psychology and in related areas of science. Public policy has reinforced this. For example, toward the end of the last century, advances in brain science began to look so promising that the United States Senate decided that it would be proper to invest large sums of money in brain research. They even decided to call the 1990s "The Decade of the Brain." Judging by some of the rapid advances in brain research, their money was well spent. I'm sure you will hear about these advances in due course.

Malcolm,

What are some of the advances that excite you?

Ben,

At the turn of this century there was particular interest and excitement about developments in techniques for imaging the brain. Researchers saw the possibility of actually seeing which areas of the brain were most active when volunteers were doing all sorts of tasks, such as looking at art, listening to music, showing maternal love, meditating and praying. Everything seemed so well set for rapid advances in the study of mind and brain that some scientists suggested that the first decade of this century should be called "The Decade of the Mind and Brain."

The largest body of scientific psychologists in North America, the American Psychological Society, with some twenty thousand members, set up a group in 2009 to discuss and write papers on where they saw the science of psychology going in the foreseeable future. They produced a fascinating report. What I found particularly interesting was that the first of the areas that they identified was the future of research in mind and brain. So don't be surprised if you get a lot of this in your courses!

I just went downstairs to make myself a cup of tea and pick up today's mail. It included a regular update I receive on research being supported by the Wellcome Foundation, the biggest funder of medical research in Britain by far. Looking through the update, I came across two reports that nicely illustrate what I suspect are some of the concerns behind your own questions. The first one looked at how levels of dopamine—a chemical in the brain involved in mediating reward, motivation and learning through reinforcement—make us more likely to opt for instant gratification rather than waiting for a more beneficial reward. Such research may enable clinicians working with children with attention deficit hyperactivity disorder (ADHD) to gain insight into how they can give the greatest help possible. This particular report also gives a good example of how giving a treatment to alleviate one condition may have undesirable effects on another. A substance called L-dopa has been used for some years to help alleviate the symptoms of Parkinson's disease, but a potential negative side effect of this treatment is that it may make people more impulsive.

The second report, I suspect, you may find more disturbing. A group of researchers at Cambridge studied teenagers who were habitually engaged in severe antisocial behavior, and they found that such individuals displayed an abnormal pattern of brain activity compared with their peers. The question arises, then: How do we judge responsibility for our actions? I suspect we shall come back to that later.

Malcolm,

I think that part of what I find a little scary is that this brain-mind science might try to explain away my faith. If it does, how can I still hold on to it?

Ben,

Good question, Ben. Judging by some of the media reports this year, and statements made by some high-profile and respected neuroscientists, I shouldn't be surprised if in the current decade we hear a lot about not just minds and brains but also about minds, brains and God(s). Indeed it has already started. During the decade of the brain, a book appeared with the provocative title *Where God Lives in the Human Brain.*[3] It was not a particularly important book as a contribution to neurology or neuroscience, but because of its provocative title and the large number of professing Christians in North America, it received wide media attention. This was followed in 2009 by another book with a similarly provocative title linking God and the brain, *How God Changes Your Brain,* written jointly by a neuroradiologist and a psychotherapist.[4] This sort of research is labeled "neurotheology." Some religious people think they can use this research to prove that God exists. Some atheists see it as showing that believing in gods is nothing but an evolutionary leftover in the way our brains developed.

But I'm talking too much about things that probably won't enter your studies until later. You'll encounter these issues in more depth later on in your studies. In the meantime, you will likely confront some challenges to your faith, as you suspect. It is difficult to avoid a knee-jerk reaction if you hear that "psychology is proving that" some of your deeply held Christian beliefs are "nothing but" wishful thinking or "nothing but" the meaningless chatter of some of your brain cells. Always remember that if such sweeping accusations are being made by nonbelievers or militant atheists, the same treatment applies to their beliefs—it is "nothing but" wishful thinking, or an attempt to avoid the challenges of Christian faith, or the random chattering of the neurons in their brains. A readable book identifying some of these issues is *Psychology Through the Eyes of Faith.*[5] If you can make time, I would have a look at it.

Malcolm,

I've been confused by the meaning of the word *mind* in different contexts. On the one hand are my psychology courses. When my lecturers talk about the mind, they never really say what they mean by it. I looked in my textbook (by David Myers) for help and noticed that near the beginning, in his chapter titled "The Biology of Mind," he launches into the topic on the assumption that we all know what is meant by "the mind."[6] But do we all mean the same thing?

On the other hand are recent Bible studies at my home church. The minister has been talking about the mind, such as what the apostle Paul meant in Romans 12:2 when he said, "be transformed by the renewal of your mind." The minister linked this individual exhortation with the group reference in Philippians 2:5, where Paul said to them, "Have this mind among yourselves, which is yours in Christ Jesus." He also pointed out that the apostle Peter wrote in his first letter, "Finally, all of you, have unity of mind, sympathy, brotherly love, a tender heart, and a humble mind" (1 Peter 3:8).

So my question is, do the biblical uses of the word *mind* relate in any straightforward way to what I'm hearing about in my psychology lectures? As far as I can see, all that my lecturers mean by *mind* is the mental processes involved in things like thinking, remembering, perceiving and so on. None of them seem to regard mind as some sort of separate entity. They use it as a shorthand for mental functions. So should I try to find links between what the Bible says about mind and what I hear in my lectures?

Ben,

I understand why you ask that question. I think the specific problem you're raising about the way the word *mind* is used is an example of a general problem of how to relate the language and statements of the Bible with language in other domains of knowledge, such as in science. In a way, this is another example of a problem faced by Christians when they were first told by scientists that the earth is rotating on its axis. Some theologians said this could not be true because it says quite clearly in Psalm 74:17 that the earth is fixed and cannot be moved. What could be clearer than that?

The problem is confounded today when we have dozens of different English translations of the Bible and we find varying words used by the different translators of the same passage of Scripture. The lesson from the past is clear: We must not try to turn the Bible into any sort of textbook of science; rather, we must be very careful to look at the language we are using. If we do that, we shall save ourselves a great deal of unnecessary anxiety and worry. And that applies in the case of the meanings of the word *mind*. Just how difficult it is to maintain this very necessary "semantic hygiene" is underlined when we remember that in the past the words *mind* and *soul* have been used interchangeably. Add to that the fact that it is only a little under a century since books were written with titles such as *Psychology in the Service of the Soul* and you can see how easy it is to get confused. So, as a rough guideline, I suggest you ask yourself, is *mind* here being used as a scientific term, as a shorthand for "the mental aspect of a psychobiological unity," for example, as used by cognitive neuroscientists, or is it being used (as most often it is in scriptural contexts) to refer to an attitude or shared set of attitudes and beliefs (e.g., Philippians 2:5 or Romans 12:2)? Almost always, the answer to your question is no—*mind* does not mean the same thing in science as in Scripture.

The temptation to mix our languages happens more easily in psychology than in other sciences. The language used in physics or chemistry or biochemistry, for example, is so clearly technical and therefore self-evidently different from everyday language, including the everyday language of the Bible. So there is no temptation to imagine that they are the same. In the case of psychology, so many of the words we use are words used in everyday discourse—for example, *thinking, remembering* and *seeing*—and therefore there is a greater tendency and temptation to confuse the words, failing to distinguish between a strictly scientific context and an everyday context. The only way to avoid muddle and pseudoconflict is eternal vigilance.

Malcolm,

Does the accelerating pace of research in psychology and neuroscience mean that all our talk about mental processes will be reduced to talk about what is happening in the brain? That seems to be a shared assumption among some of our lecturers, if only we could understand how our mental processes depend upon (and quite a lot of them seem to assume originate in and reduce to) the specific workings of different parts of our brains.

For example, in my evolutionary psychology lectures we were told a lot about what is called "mind-reading behavior"—how in our social interaction with other people, we tend to try to read what our friends are thinking ("read their minds"). It seems there is evidence of similar behavior in monkeys. But we were told that this capacity for mind reading depends upon the functioning of a particular group of cells in the brain.

So my question is, how do you think about the relation of the mind and the brain in a way that ultimately does not reduce the mind to the brain and reduce psychology to neuroscience and evolutionary biology? And how have views about the relation of mind and brain changed over the centuries?

Ben,

Trying to relate mind and brain has a very long history. Several millennia ago, wiser men than us were thinking about this. They were aware, for example, that if you think exciting thoughts, you may experience thumping in your chest; think peaceful thoughts and your heart stops thumping. On the basis of that subjective evidence, the obvious place to localize your mind was in your heart. The philosopher Empedocles in the fifth century B.C. reasserted the notion that the soul, which was the Greek word for the mind, was to be found in the heart and blood. With good reason, this was called the "cardiovascular theory." His views didn't go unchallenged. Around the same time, Alcmaeon of Croton claimed that mental functions are located in the brain. His view was dubbed the "encephalic view." Over the next two thousand years, these two theories competed. The great physician Hippocrates lived sometime between 460 and 360 B.C. and made the brain the interpreter of consciousness as well as a mediator of feelings. His theory was dubbed the "encephalic theory of mind." In his book *On the Sacred Disease,* he deals extensively with epilepsy.

In the fourth century B.C., the conflict between the encephalic and cardiovascular theories was well exemplified by the opposing views of Plato and Aristotle. Plato seemed to want it both ways. He located the immortal soul in the marrow of the head, presumably the brain, but located the passions between the neck and the midriff, presumably the heart. Aristotle unambiguously localized the mind in the heart, but he still had a role for the brain. Being a good biologist, he decided it must serve some function, and noticing that it was moist to the touch, he concluded that it refrigerated the blood! Aristotle's views were passed on to the Stoic philosophers and then to the so-called church fathers. Tertullian, for example, adopted Aristotle's views. The encephalic view survived through Galen, one of Rome's outstanding physicians.

In the fourth century A.D., Nemesius, Bishop of Emesa in Syria who claimed to be a follower of Galen, produced yet another new theory of the physical basis of the mind. He distinguished three different mental faculties, as he called them—sense and imagination, thought and judgment, and memory. He localized each of these in the different ventricles of the brain. Now there were three different groups of partisans, each supporting different views of the mind-body relationship: the encephalic, the cardiovascular and the ventricular theories.

It is interesting that at the time that Galileo was bringing forward his evidence to challenge the widely held cosmological beliefs in the Christian church, his contemporary Vesalius was using the results of his careful dissections of the human body, including the brain (which had previously been forbidden on theological grounds), and producing empirical data that raised questions about mind-body theories. Vesalius dissected the bodies not only of humans but also of apes, dogs, horses, sheep and other animals and found that they all possessed ventricles in the brain. According to contemporary Christian anthropology, these were where the uniquely human soul or mind were located. However, this evidence for the presence of ventricles in animals produced a major blow against the ventricular theory for the unique existence of the soul in humans. By the time you get to Shakespeare's era, you find there are at least three different theories in circulation about the mind-body relationship, and Shakespeare refers to each of these in his various plays.

I'm afraid that's a long digression, but I just wanted you to understand that this question of the relation of the mind or soul to the brain and body has a very long history. And the point of looking at history is that if we take it seriously, it warns us over and over again against the dangers of reading into the data beliefs that we brought from some other sphere of knowledge, such as Christian belief. The temptation to read *into* the text of Scripture is always with us. I was reminded of this very recently in an email I received from theologian Tom Wright. He said that we find it all too easy "to allow our traditions to echo back off the surface of the text that is trying to tell us something else," and that "all too often the word 'biblical' itself has been shrunk so that it only now means 'according to our own tradition, which we assume to be biblical.'"[7]

Malcolm,

Obviously this is something you've thought a lot about! I appreciated your emphasizing the danger of reading into data our preconceived ideas, whether the data is the text of Scripture or the data gathered by science. I can see how our preconceived ideas that are appropriate in one context may be either inappropriate or wrong, or both, in another context. In light of the history you outlined for me of the mind-brain connection, how do we best think about the relationship between mental processes and the brain today?

Ben,

You say you want to know how best to think about the relationship of the mind and the brain today, which really means you want a snapshot of what is currently happening. I'll tell you what I think, but I warn you that it may all change tomorrow. Again, I think you can only really understand where we are today by taking a very brief look at the more recent past.

Neuropsychology, as a separate subdiscipline, really only took off after the Second World War. In part it was as a result of attempts to help returning servicemen who had suffered localized brain damage, often from gunshot wounds to the head. Underlying the approach was the belief that the different kinds of deficits in mental functioning and behavior might arise from very specific and localized brain lesions.

By the 1960s and 1970s the new discipline of neuropsychology received considerable help when researchers no longer had to rely on either postmortem studies of the brain or knowing something about the actual position of entry and exit of a bullet wound to the head, because now, due to the invention of what was called x-ray computed tomography, or CT scan, it was possible to see the damaged structures of the living brain in a noninvasive manner. In the following decades there were spectacular advances in these noninvasive imaging techniques. First there was positron emission tomography (PET) scanning, then there was functional magnetic resonance imaging (fMRI). Both of these monitored changes in local blood flow in the brain related to metabolism and chemical and electrical activities of neurons and glia cells. It became feasible to begin to match deficits in particular cognitive operations resulting from localized brain damage with the activation of the same selective cortical regions in the normal brain when carrying out cognitive operations. Most recently additional information has become available by using a technique that produces a temporary functional inactivation of selected areas of the cortex using what is called transcranial magnetic stimulation (TMS). I suspect you will hear quite a lot about some of these in your lectures.

The overall picture that emerged was that it became possible to map, in much greater detail, changes in mental processes to verified changes in the structure and activity of different parts of the brain. The result: every new advance seemed to tighten the link between mind and brain.

But the course of research never runs smoothly. Just when cognitive neuroscientists began to feel that they were getting a better understanding of the principal brain systems, a paper appeared in the *Annals of the New York Academy of Sciences* titled "The Brain's Default Network." Three distinguished Harvard researchers—Randy Buchner, Jessica Andrews-Hanna and Daniel Schacter—reviewed thirty years of brain imaging research, which they said "had converged to define the brain's default network—a novel and only recently appreciated brain system that participates in the internal modes of cognition."[8] They trace out the interconnections of this system and discuss how knowing something about its structure and function gives new understanding for mental disorders including autism, schizophrenia and Alzheimer's disease. So we learn the importance of continually asking questions. There are always new things to discover about the unbelievably complex systems and subsystems in our mysterious brains and how they embody and facilitate our mental life.

Having said that, I hasten to add that not all psychologists followed the same approach. Some preferred to think of the brain as an information-processing system and saw cognitive tasks as being normally carried out by sets of discreet, separable and relatively autonomous information-processing components, sometimes called modules. Some of the champions of this kind of approach prided themselves in eschewing any attempt to correlate a pattern of cognitive deficits under examination with the causative changes in cerebral organization. These people called themselves cognitive neuropsychologists. This approach to research led to the widely accepted view, for the past thirty years, that the functional organization of the human cerebral cortex could best be understood in terms of differences between the left and right cerebral hemispheres. The left hemisphere is seen as specialized for language, logical thinking, mathematical and analytical processing, and the serial processing of sensory information. The right hemisphere is seen as specialized for emotional expression, intuitive thinking, recognizing faces and musical sequences, parallel processing and visual-spatial encoding. In short, the left is verbal, logical, rule bound; the right, intuitive and creative.

Consult any textbook of psychology and it will likely give you that picture of brain hemispheres specialization. Much of this thinking remains well founded, but very recently, in October 2011, the foundations of this approach were shaken in a paper written by three of today's leading cognitive neuroscientists—Gregoire Borst, William Thompson and Stephen Kosslyn. They argue, with detailed supporting evidence and literature reviews, that "a top-bottom divide, rather than a left-right divide, is a more fruitful way to organize human cortical brain functions."[9] I'll return to their paper in a moment; for now, the point is to remind you that research is moving forward at an ever-accelerating pace as new techniques such as functional brain imaging are refined and become more widely available. This radical new way of dichotomizing brain function should warn everyone of the dangers of trying to use what is seen as a well-established, widely accepted view as the final answer. More serious are attempts to use a particular view of brain science—in this instance, of left-brain/right-brain differences—to support a view of how society in general has advanced, using the accepted model to characterize and critique what has been happening in other fields of learning.

For example, in a recent book titled *The Master and His Emissary*,[10] psychiatrist Iain McGilchrist has written engagingly about the left-right hemisphere differences and how they may help us to understand some of the wider trends in western thinking in recent years. Picking up on this theme, Tom Wright sees aspects of biblical scholarship as predominantly left-hemisphere, preoccupied with "microscopic analysis of details." "Facts," Wright says, "are left-brain business." Wright urges us that "only when the detailed left-brain analysis can be relocated as the emissary to the right-wing intuition, with its rich world of metaphor, narrative and above all imagination, can the discipline [biblical scholarship] become healthy again."[11]

I do not doubt that all that Wright says in comment and criticism of some aspects of biblical scholarship is true, and I am not competent to judge, but I would be careful of seeming to tie my views on this topic to what is thought to be the last word on hemispheric specialization. Wright's views convince me without the support of changing views of brain functioning.

What I mean is, as you will have found in a few pages from David Myers's *Psychology (10th edition),* which I know you use, the story is more complex. For example, a caption to an illustration on page 79 reads, "Pop psychology's idea of hemispheric specialization. Alas, reality is more complex." The image is an artist's impression of an open skull. On the left side of the exposed brain there are rows of people working hard at their desks; on the right side are people enjoying artistic and cultural pastimes, exercising their emotions. His point is that there is much truth in the rough characterization of hemisphere differences, but the real story is much more complex.

My concern is not only that "reality is more complex," but also that the views that have prevailed for more than four decades and have been taken over by pop psychology now begin to look as if they may not be the best way of characterizing cerebral specialization after all. In 2003 Toga and Thompson published a paper in the very prestigious journal *Nature Reviews Neuroscience* that I think nicely characterizes views that were held for three decades, though even they warn about not overstating the case. For example, in their conclusion they write, "The pattern of asymmetries varies with handedness, gender and age, and with a variety of genetic factors and hormonal influences."[12]

I'll return to the paper published in *American Psychologist*—where the authors argue for a top-down divide of brain functions rather than a left-right divide—to further underline the need for caution. The first two sentences of the abstract encapsulate my concerns. The authors write, "Traditionally, characterizations of the macrolevel functional organization of the human cerebral cortex have focused on the left and right cerebral hemispheres. *However, the idea of left brain versus right brain functions has been shown to be an oversimplification.*"[13]

In the early part of this paper the authors note in detail how the left and right hemispheres were conceived as specialized in particular ways, concluding that, "Such oversimplified views of hemispheric specialization has led to the concept of individuals who have left or right brain personalities."[14]

The lesson from these research examples is this: If you are using a model from science as a metaphor, be careful not to seem to tie your theological or other nonscientific beliefs to science, which by its nature is changing.

Today things have moved a little further and the emphasis is on what is called "cognitive neuroscience." I suspect that in due course this will supersede the term *neuropsychology,* but we shall have to wait and see. Even if the old labels disappear, the aims of neuropsychological research will remain—how best to understand the relationship between the mind and behavior on the one hand, and the brain on the other. This I suspect will remain the ultimate goal of the neurosciences.

Malcolm,

Thank you for bringing me up to date. I've noticed that some of our psychology courses make no reference at all to the brain. The lecturers argue that their task as psychologists is to try to understand human psychological processes and to make testable models of those. I can understand that, but since I'm also doing neuroscience, I want to know how best to understand how psychological processes relate to the physical processes in the brain.

Ben,

I think the first thing to clarify is that it makes no sense to speak as if the only true reality is a physical reality—namely, the brain—and that therefore brain language must always take precedence over mind language. A brief moment of reflection reminds us that we couldn't even talk about brains unless we had the mental concepts of brain, mind and behavior. So mind language in that sense takes priority. I personally don't think it makes sense to try to say that a mental or a physical description is more important—the question is, more important for what? If you are a psychotherapist, the psychological concepts, most of the time, are clearly the ones of primary concern.

I prefer to think about mind and brain as two aspects of one complex system. In this sense, in complementary fashion, mental activity and behavior depend on the physically determinate operations of the brain, itself a physicochemical system. When that system goes wrong or is disordered, there are changes in its capabilities for running the system that we describe as the mind or mental activity. (In that sense the psychotherapist will also be alert to any possible identifiable brain changes that she ought to be aware of.) Likewise, if the mind or the mental activity results in behavior of particular kinds, this in turn may result in temporary or chronic changes in the physicochemical makeup and activity of the brain, its physical substrate. Thus this ever-tightening link does not minimize the importance of the mind or the brain in this unitary complex system.

My own thinking was greatly helped by that of the distinguished neuroscientist, neuropsychologist and Nobel prizewinner Professor Roger Sperry, who emphasized the importance of conscious mental life. Far from ruling out causal power to the mind, he underlined that the mind has such power. He wrote, "Consciousness exerts potent causal effects on the interplay of cerebral operations." He went so far as to say that the mind plays a kind of executive role: "In the position of top command at the highest levels in the hierarchy of brain organization, the subjective properties were seen to exert control over the biophysical and chemical activities at subordinate levels."[15]

Picking up on Roger Sperry's way of thinking about the relation of mind and brain, you will find that in recent years there's been a lot of talk about the relative contributions of "top-down" (meaning, the mental aspects) and "bottom-up" (meaning, the neural or physical or biological substrates of mental life). There is wide agreement that any attempt to do justice to our mysterious human nature, recognizing our conscious experience and at the same time understanding how it can be changed by damage to its physical substrates, must do full justice to both these aspects of reality. In talking about mind-brain relations, you need to be very alert to those using an analogy—such as the brain as a computer with its hardware and software—as if it might actually solve the mind-brain problem, when all it does is describe it in another way.

To understand how the human brain handles our thoughts, emotions and actions would solve the perennial mind-brain problem. More than a century ago the Harvard physiologist and psychologist William James had no doubt that to achieve a solution to this would make all previous achievements pale into insignificance. William James's sober assessment was taken up by one of today's most distinguished philosophers of mind, Thomas Nagel, who writes, "As far as we can tell, our mental lives and those of other creatures, including subjective experiences, are strongly connected with and perhaps strictly dependent on physical events in our brains and on the physical interaction of our bodies with the rest of the physical world." But he has no doubts that "we have to reject conceptual reduction of the mental to the physical," and he acknowledges that "the mind-body problem is difficult enough so that we should be suspicious of attempts to solve it with the concepts and methods developed to account for very different kinds of things. Instead we should expect theoretical progress in this area to require a major conceptual revolution."[16] Nagel believes that that will require a change in thinking at least as radical as relativity theory was in physics.

The temptation to slip into unthinking reductionism is always there. It is not an issue that divides Christians and non-Christians. Neurologist and neuroscientist Raymond Tallis, who has highlighted the dangers of what he calls "biologism,"[17] describes himself as an atheist humanist. He has a shared concern with religious people of the need to guard against the abuse of science and its misrepresentation, at times, in the popular media. He has offered a trenchant critique of reductionists who believe that our greatest human conceptual abilities can be reduced to the neural firings in our brains. He calls them "neuromaniacs." He is equally critical of those who seek to minimize human differences from other animals by, on the one hand, anthropomorphizing animals, or, on the other hand, "animalizing" humans, in entirely unjustified ways. This he calls "Darwinitis." Each of these, in different ways, as the title of his book *Aping Mankind: Neuromania, Darwinitis and the Misrepresentation of Humanity* suggests, has the effect of misrepresenting humanity. Those of us who are neuroscientists and psychologists and who are concerned about this misuse, as well as the proper use, of science will continue to take his warnings seriously.

Another current champion for psychological science has just reinforced Tallis's message. At the 24th annual convention of the American Psychological Society in 2012, Carol Tavris—this time not a neuroscientist but a social psychologist—commented, "I have spent many years lobbing hand grenades at psychobabble—that wonderful assortment of pop psychology and ideas that permeate our culture in spite of having no means of empirical support." She went on to add, "Today, however, we face an even greater challenge because in this era of medical-pharmaceutical-industrial complex, where psychobabble goes, can biobunk be far behind?"[18]

She believes that the public has a preference for what she calls "neat" biological explanations instead of "messy" psychological ones, and this has led scientists to search for genes that explain behavior. She is not negative about this biomedical revolution. What she is concerned about is the public perception that biomedical explanations are infallible. She notes how the public is mesmerized by stunning colored images of brains without knowing what it all means—it all looks so scientific!

One thing is clear. The evidence all points to the need to recognize that we are each a psychobiological unity and that this unity can be disrupted by disease or accidental damage to the biological aspects that in turn may be modified, in a reciprocal manner, by the psychological aspects.

Malcolm,

What did you mean by saying, "if the mind or the mental activity results in behavior of particular kinds, this in turn may result in temporary or chronic changes in the physicochemical makeup and activity of the brain, its physical substrate"? Do you really mean that the things that I think about and the things that I habitually do can be having an effect on my brain?

Ben,

Yes, I do. Let me explain.

Evidence in recent years has been steadily accumulating that points to the intimate relationships between mind, brain and behavior. The emerging consensus on this is illustrated by the comments of leading neurologist Antonio Damasio, who believes that the old distinction between diseases of brain and mind is an unfortunate cultural inheritance that nevertheless still permeates society and medicine.[19] His views were echoed by a recent president of the Royal College of psychiatrists in Britain, Robert Kendell, who believed that the distinction between mental and physical illness was ill founded and not compatible with contemporary understanding of disease.[20]

One very widely publicized recent study on this topic illustrates the kind of evidence that has been collected. You've probably at some time been in a taxi and have been amazed at the way in which the driver seemed to know every little side road in the metropolis. Before they can qualify as taxi drivers, they have to do a two-year training course. Some researchers in

London decided to use modern brain scanning techniques to study the brains of these taxi drivers and a group of matched controls. They studied a part of the brain that is already known to be intimately involved in memory, the hippocampus. They found convincing evidence that the hippocampus, both in size and shape, changed over the course of taxi-driver training and was significantly different in size and shape from the matched controls. They argued from their results that the brain has a capacity for what they called "local plastic change . . . in response to environmental demands."[21] There have been a number of other studies since then that all confirm this picture of how if you selectively mobilize specific brain systems in a sustained manner, that can be shown to modify the brain structures.

Eleanor Maguire, the lead researcher in the London taxi drivers study, has recently been showing that experience can indeed change the brain in very specific ways. Like all good researchers, she has been publishing further exciting findings, now about the way in which memories, such as those of the spatial maps of the taxi drivers, are actually encoded in the brain.

In her more recent experiments she asked volunteers to view three short films and to memorize what they saw. The films were about everyday things that a woman might do in a typical urban street. The volunteers were asked to recall the films while they were lying inside an fMRI scanner. A computer program then studied the patterns in the volunteers' brains, and the researchers were asked to identify, if they could, which film the volunteer was recalling purely by looking at the pattern of their brain activity. The remarkable thing was that it was possible to tell which film they were thinking of.

This research also showed that in the typical brain areas involved in this study, you could identify the precise circuits used to recall one particular memory trace in an individual's brain down to a resolution of just over one cubic millimeter. This revealed much more detailed information about how the hippocampus worked. So localization in the brain is quite remarkable.

The picture that is generally held today is that we need simultaneously to remember that cognitive processes are embedded in the brain and, at the same time, that they also have scope to alter the brain, as in the case of the taxi drivers. Maguire's most recently publicized work, in December 2011, further clarifies and confirms her earlier findings. With Katharine Woollett, she has conducted a longitudinal study examining seventy-nine male trainee

London taxi drivers at the start of their training and then again three to four years later just after qualification, as well as thirty-one male control participants. Some of those who trained failed to qualify, and others did not complete the training. The main finding was that those who did the training and qualified showed significant changes in brain structures, while those who failed to qualify and the controls did not. The authors acknowledge, "It could be that there are inherited factors that feed into individual differences in spatial memory and navigation ability." They note that these recent findings raise afresh the perennial "nature vs. nurture" questions.[22]

Another example of this was shown in a study that used cognitive behavior therapy. This is a technique that has been successfully used to help patients with persistent phobias, such as spider phobia, that can be very disabling. Over a period of time these patients are able to become more and more familiar with spiders, first through looking at pictures of them and then gradually seeing the real thing and eventually actually touching them. The net result is that by the systematic modification of how they think about spiders and how they behave toward them, they are able to overcome their phobia. The researchers in this case used modern brain scanning techniques and demonstrated how, over the course of the cognitive behavior therapy, the areas in the brain that initially were extremely active whenever spiders were seen, steadily diminished in activity until eventually the activity was at the level of a person who had no spider phobia. In effect, by modifying thinking and behavior, brain processes were also modified.[23] Hence the use of the term *top-down effect.*

Malcolm,

Some of the research examples you referenced are fascinating! But I still have questions: What kind of view makes sense of all this evidence that points to the intimate relationship between what we think, how we behave and the detailed structures of our brains? And will all the psychological descriptions eventually be reduced to neural processes?

Ben,

I'm afraid there are no simple answers. The easy approach would be to say that all mental activity will ultimately be reduced down to brain activity.

Some people have done that. Francis Crick, arguably the greatest biologist of the twentieth century, seemed to take that view, although at times he backed off from it a bit, realizing, I suppose, that it meant that his own brilliant discoveries and his reporting of them would become nothing more than the chattering of neurons. Other Nobel laureates who have studied brain processes have taken different views. Sir John Eccles had no doubt that the primary reality is consciousness and everything else derives from that. A more recent laureate, Gerald Edelman, argued that consciousness is "efficacious," and is not an epiphenomenon. Yet another laureate, Roger Sperry, whom I mentioned earlier, argued very strongly for a model that he thought best fit the evidence, and that was to put full weight on the top-down effect as well as on the traditional upward microdeterminism, which is happening at the level of neurons and of the atoms and molecules of which the neurons are composed. Sir Roger Penrose, an Oxford mathematician, had no doubt that consciousness is a phenomenon through which the universe's very existence is made known. In a word, it is stupid to pretend that consciousness and mental life are unimportant.

Various people have tried in various ways to formalize all this in succinct statements. You may come across some of them. It seems to me that certain things stand out. As I said earlier, we are a psychobiological unity. The evidence currently available demonstrates a remarkable *interdependence* between what is happening in the physical substrates in the brain and body, and what is happening in terms of mental processes. This interdependence seems to be evident every time the studies take place—in other words, for me, they seem to be a part of the way the world is, so I tend to think of this interdependence as what I call *intrinsic* interdependence, or naturally inherent. It also seems to me that we cannot reduce the mental to the physical any more than we can reduce the physical to the mental. In this sense there is an important *duality* that we need to recognize between the mental and physical, and I don't believe this duality requires us to believe in two kinds of substances or a dualism of substance, and that makes me a "dual-aspect monist."

3

How Free Am I?

Free Will and Determinism

Malcolm,

Almost everything you have told me about the relation of brain and mind points to such close links between them that I wonder whether it makes sense anymore to believe that we have free will. Since the brain is a physical system made up of atoms and molecules, how can there be any room for the top-down processes you have described that enable us to make choices and decisions? I believe that I make my own decisions and execute my own actions, so I struggle with this idea that new research may indicate that we don't have free will. Can you help me?

Ben,

You are in good company. These are not new questions. Leading scientific academies in Britain and the U.S.A. are alert to these questions and have organized forums to work on them. For example, the Royal Society in London, noting that in some people's minds neuroscience has already cast doubt on the idea of free will, brought together neuroscientists and lawyers to discuss neuroscience and the law.[1]

In the U.S. a number of universities already teach courses on the interface between neuroscience and the law. The Chicago-based MacArthur Foundation has invested several million dollars to fund research in this area.[2] And all this is not speculating about what might happen in the future. Already evidence from fMRI has been used in successfully persuading an Italian judge to commute the sentence of a woman convicted of murder, following the submission of brain imaging and genetic evidence.

In 2009 Stefania Albertani pleaded guilty to murdering her sister and burying her corpse. She was sentenced to life imprisonment. A report in the journal *Nature* records how Albertani's legal defense called a cognitive neuroscientist as a witness. He demonstrated that, compared with ten healthy control subjects, Albertani had structural brain abnormalities, including the anterior cingulate gyrus (known to be implicated in inhibition) and the insular (known to be associated with aggression). In addition, a geneticist gave evidence that the woman has genes predisposing her to violence. This included the MAOA so-called warrior gene, the implication being that her body was producing lower levels of an enzyme involved in regulating neurotransmitter levels. Given this new evidence, the judge reduced Albertani's sentence to twenty years.[3]

In the early days of phrenology—the search for links between mind and brain through studying the bumps on the head—the suggestion that some sort of a unified theory of mind and body was possible was seen as a threat to the classic notion of free will. The Catholic Church in Austria, holding what was called the Thomistic theory that the soul was above and separate from matter as the cause of its life, saw the notion of the union of body and mind as a challenge to the clergy's responsibility to guide Catholics toward proper moral conduct. The result was that leading phrenologist Franz Joseph Gall was forced to leave Vienna and flee to Paris. Fortunately those of us who today see this very tight link between mind and brain or body and soul do not face the same risks of having to flee the country!

But it is a genuine issue. Neurologists see people with brain tumors who seem to have lost control over their actions. They "lie, damage property, and in extreme rare cases, commit murder. . . . The individuals simply lose the ability to control impulses or anticipate the consequences of choices." One psychiatrist, specializing in behavioral disorders linked to brain disorders, asked the question, "If one's actions are governed by how well the brain is working, does it mean we have less free will than we think?"[4]

You won't be surprised to know that there is already an enormous body of literature on this. The solutions proposed to justify our conviction that we have free will fall into two groups. On the one hand, there are the "compatabilists," who argue that determinism is compatible with free will. On the other hand are the "libertarians," who argue that free will requires a fundamental indeterminism in nature, and in particular in the way the brain functions. In order to justify the required indeterminism, most of those who invoke the libertarian view depend heavily on what in physics is called Heisenberg Uncertainty.

For you and me as Christians, there is the further question of how each of these approaches relates to what the Bible teaches about our responsibility to choose wisely. How many sermons have you heard where texts such as, "Choose you this day whom you will serve" and "If anyone is willing to . . . then . . ." are invoked to remind us of the choices we must make? But are we free to choose? Continuing research will shed more light on this debate.

Malcolm,

I'm not familiar with Heisenberg's Uncertainty Principle. Can you describe it for me? Why is it important in these discussions of free will and the activity of the brain?

Ben,

Basically Heisenberg's Uncertainty Principle says there is a fundamental limit to how precisely certain pairs of physical quantities can be measured. The pair most often talked about are the momentum and the position of a particle. There is no limit to how precisely the momentum alone of the electron can be measured, nor its position alone, but it seems that any gain in the precision of measurement of one member of the pair is inevitably offset by less precision for the other member of the pair. I hasten to add that Heisenberg Uncertainty is not relevant to large objects like tennis balls, but it is extremely relevant to microscopic entities like electrons.

Neuroscientist Peter Clarke has written about how some philosophers have seized on Heisenberg Uncertainty to argue against physical determinism. He conjures up a rather nice picture when he says that they treat it "as a kind of cloud cover in which small perturbations can occur unnoticed by the watchful eye of nature's laws." On this view the top-down effects can occur hidden within the cloud cover of Heisenberg Uncertainty. Clarke notes, however, that "according to standard quantum physics, such hidden effects are assumed to be random, but the unconventional proposal of quantum libertarianism is that they are nonrandom, directed by the mind (or soul)."[5]

Sir John Eccles, whom I have mentioned already and who held an essentially dualist view of the relation of the mind to the brain, saw Heisenberg Uncertainty as a way of allowing the mind to modify the functions of the brain without violating any physical laws. Eccles saw the top-down decision-making processes as able to influence the electrical activity of the brain at the junctions between neurons in the cerebral cortex, known as the synapses. Others disagreed and argued that the Heisenberg effects are much too small to affect even the most sensitive physical changes in the brain, such as the concentration of synaptic calcium. But this is getting very technical. My own impression is that those who attempt to free the brain from determinism using Heisenberg Uncertainty have yet to convince fellow scientists, who are aware of the smallness of the uncertainty involved, of the cogency of their case. But for now, the jury is still out.

Malcolm,

So how can you still maintain your belief in free will while arguing so strongly for the ever-tightening links between mind and brain?

Ben,

I will try to answer your question, but I apologize in advance because I'll have to get a little bit technical again. Let's start where we left off, talking about the laws of physics. There is increasing evidence that leads us to believe that systems made up of elements obeying the laws of physics nevertheless embody forms of causation that seem to transcend the determinism of these atomic, physical and chemical laws. The two concepts that we come across most often in these discussions are *emergence* and a more sophisticated version of what I called "top-down effects," which is actually called *top-down causation.* If you put these things together, a scientifically plausible picture emerges of one possible way in which mental processes and moral agencies can remain the real causes of behavior even though embodied within a physical/biological system.

The concept of emergence helps to describe how complex entities like biological organisms can have properties that do not exist within the elements, such as the molecules, that make up the organism. Even a simple organism like an amoeba, which is a complex organization of molecules, manifests properties that don't exist in the molecules themselves. The behavior of the amoeba depends upon the current state of the organization of the molecules, not the molecules themselves. In this sense the activity of the amoeba is an example of an emergent property.

In the scientific literature you'll find that another term for emergence is *dynamical systems theory*. Application of this theory helps to explain how new causal properties, such as the behavior of humans, can emerge in complex systems characterized by a high level of nonlinear interactions between their elements. A perfect example of this is the human cerebral cortex. The millions of neurons and their millions of interconnections form an ideal dynamical system. From this point of view, the elements of human neurobiology in the form of the cerebral cortex produce the cognitive properties of a whole person.

One of the fascinating things about these complex systems is that they manifest novelty. I don't understand all the details, but my reading tells me that even in small-scale mathematical models of dynamical systems, no two runs of the same system model ever come out exactly the same. These systems are almost trivial in size compared with the complexity of the human brain, and that helps us to explain and understand how the physical brain produces emergent properties unexplainable in terms of the operation of the laws of physics, chemistry and even of neurons.

These higher-level emergent properties are very similar to what I have said about top-down effects. Looked at in this way, thinking, believing and remembering can be seen as represented by shifting patterns in the dynamical neural system, and these patterns create top-down influences on the lower-level neurophysiological phenomena that are the substrate of, and that support, the mental activities themselves.

What this amounts to is that the description of the mind-brain in terms of its physical properties is compatible with a description of the same system in terms of mental concepts like thinking, believing and remembering. *Both levels of description are necessary to give a full account of the whole unbelievably complex system.* You will also have noticed that the very terms in which we are able to debate and discuss these issues are themselves emergent properties of the whole system. Without these higher-level mental conceptual tools, we cannot even talk about and debate these issues, and in this sense, any attempt to reduce them to the chattering of interacting neurons at once empties them of all logic and meaning.

4

Determinism, Genetics and the "God Gene"

Malcolm,

While we're talking about determinism, I notice that you said nothing at all about things like genetic determinism and environmental determinism. After reading the chapter titled "Nature, Nurture and Human Diversity" in our David Myers textbook, I'm convinced about the shaping of our behavior by our genetic makeup.[1]

Added to this, one of our psychology lecturers this week gave us an introductory lecture on genetics. He said we needed to know about this because a lot of important discoveries have been made in the field of genetic psychology. I found it a bit worrying. The lecturer seemed to suggest rather strongly that all of us are much more determined than I thought we were, by things like genetic makeup and, in particular, the makeup of our brains. Most Christian preachers I hear speak as if we are all equally free to become Christians when we hear the gospel. But after learning about the genetic influence on our behavior and hearing about recent discoveries of a "God gene," I wonder if that's true. Or are some of us more likely to become religious because of our genetic makeup? On a more personal level, are you and I Christians because we happen to be genetically predisposed that way?

Sorry, that's a lot of questions, but you can see what is going through my mind.

Ben,

Your questions about possible genetic influences on whether someone is religious or not are much in the news at present. Today, with the intense search for the genetic basis of some crippling diseases, its not surprising that it spills over into media speculation about whether there is a gene for everything, including being religious.

Since you said you are attending lectures on genetics and psychology, you will have heard about research into whether personality characteristics are determined by an individual's "gene type." The human genome project, now into its third decade, continues to report discoveries of, for example, obesity genes, a criminal gene, a novelty gene and so on. Media headline stories tell us that the way to understand all our human behavior will ultimately be through our DNA, if we only knew it.

Genetic manipulations certainly can produce changes in behavior. For example, just before the turn of the century, Princeton neuroscientists reported how they had genetically modified mice, changing synaptic functions between cells in the brain to markedly improve the learning ability of their animals. The media at once speculated and asked whether similar techniques may in due time be applied to humans and, more specifically, to children with learning difficulties, as well as to those at the other end of life who develop memory problems.

When the Princeton study story broke, the late distinguished Harvard scientist Stephen J. Gould noted how the media interpretation was that scientists had demonstrated "the IQ gene." He remarked that the media treatment of their dramatic findings was a very good illustration of what he called "the labeling fallacy." He pointed out that complex organisms are not simply the sum of their genes, nor do genes alone build particular items of anatomy or behavior by themselves. He illustrated what he meant by "the labeling fallacy" by referring to the occasion in 1996 when scientists reported the discovery of a "gene for novelty-seeking" behavior. At that time this was regarded as a good thing. In 1997, however, another study found a link between the same gene and the propensity for heroin addiction. So Stephen Gould asked the question, "Did the 'good gene' for enhanced exploration become the 'bad gene' for addictive tendencies?" The biochemistry may be the same, but context and background matter.[2]

Another example is the perennial question, which has recently been linked to genetics, of why some people are left-handed. The riddle of why about 10 percent of children are born left-handed remains. Hand asymmetry is related to brain asymmetry—and that is not at all well understood.

Though brain asymmetries exist in our closest primate relatives, there is an emerging consensus that the human brain is more profoundly asymmetric. We know that handedness runs in families, but as Dr. Daniel Geschwind, professor of human genetics, neurology and psychiatry at UCLA, comments, "Handedness has a genetic basis, but like other complex traits—height, weight—it is complex. It's not a single gene that leads to it. There's a strong environmental component, too."[3]

I suspect that behind your question there may have been a further one: "If it's genetic, then what can you do about it anyway?" You will know from your lectures that research aimed at better understanding whether genetic factors produce personal individual differences explores the interaction between a developing organism and its environment. To study this in humans, the researchers compare identical and nonidentical twins. Such studies look at correlations to provide measures of similarity between twins, from the most correlated (1.00) to the least (0.00). Such correlations are found to be highest for structural and physiological variables, such as eye color; in the mid range, but somewhat higher, for mental ability than for personality; and fairly low for interests. A typical finding of the correlations of personality variables for monozygotic twins reared together (MZT) and apart (MZA) taken from the Minnesota study of twins reared apart shows that the correlations on personality traits at adulthood differ little—0.50 for the twins reared apart and 0.49 for the twins reared together.[3]

Some studies have examined the so-called big five distinguishable personality traits: (1) extroversion, dominance; (2) agreeableness, likeability, friendliness; (3) conscientiousness, conformity, will to achieve; (4) emotional stability (with anxiety and neuroticism as opposites); (5) culture, intellect, openness to experience. Results from studies of extroversion come from five large twins studies with sample sizes ranging from 475 to 12,777 pairs, an unusually large database, and are expressed normally in the form of correlation coefficients. The correlations for the monozygotic (identical twin) pairs range from 0.46 to 0.65 and to the dizygotic (nonidentical) same-sex pairs from 0.13 to 0.28, with the monozygotic-dizygotic differences showing a clear genetic effect. When all the data from twins (reared together and apart) and from adoption studies are collated, genes account for 35 to 39 percent of the individual variation in extroversion. So while it had been assumed that environment accounts for much of the family resemblance in personality, most of the studies showed the effect of shared environment to be close to zero. The general consensus at the moment seems to be that when you're talking about things like personality characteristics, it is likely that they have a complex polygenetic basis. Religiosity is so complex a concept that it is normally regarded as a personality characteristic. That being so, it would, on my view, be very surprising if there were a single "religiosity" gene.

Malcolm,

If there isn't a single religiosity gene, what are the most influential factors that have been studied regarding what makes a person religious or not?

Ben,

Leading twin researcher Lindon Eaves has gathered evidence about genetic and social influences on religion. Reviewing this material in 2004 he concluded, regarding what he called "religious affiliation," that "the correlation between twins is purely environmental in origin."[4] But there is a bit more to the story. Eaves also asked the question, What about something like church attendance as distinct from religious affiliation? Behind this question there was a suggestion that maybe there is a personality factor at work here—the tendency to "self-transcendence"—and Eaves and his colleagues wondered whether this might have an effect on, so to speak, the outworking of the nominal religious affiliation as shown in the likelihood of attending church.

In one study Eaves used a Temperament and Character Inventory in which self-transcendence is defined as the "capacity to reach out beyond oneself and discover or make meaning of experience through broadened perspectives and behavior."[5] In the study carried out on Australian twins, there were, among the fifteen items selected to represent the "self-transcendence" construct, many relating to spiritual beliefs and experience, as distinct from those relating more specifically to beliefs in God and formal religious practices.

The Australian data confirmed a significant correlation between self-transcendence and church attendance. Eaves concluded that there is "a small but significant role of genetic factors (15 to 35 percent of the total variation, depending on sex and nationality) in the creation of individual differences in church attendance."[6]

Another way of looking at this is to ask how a specific kind of top-down effect, such as the effect of religious beliefs and practices, might modify the outworking of genetic influences. A Dutch study of adolescents and young adult twins who had a problem with what is called "behavioral disinhibition" (the seeming inability, at times, to control one's behavior) shed some light on this question. Researchers confirmed that religious upbringing, entirely non-genetic, showed a very large share of environmental effect on twin resemblance. However, the most important result for our present discussion was in the pattern of twin correlations for behavioral disinhibition. When they looked at the twin pairs who had had a religious upbringing and those who had not, they found that in the pairs who had not had a religious upbringing, genetic effects, in terms of expressed behavioral disinhibition, are much more marked than in pairs who did have a religious upbringing. The researchers showed that the expression of genetic differences is not fixed but depends on the environmental context, in this case on family religion in which the genotypes are embedded. The more permissive environment of a nonreligious family facilitated the expression of the genetic defects, which were still present but nevertheless were unexpressed in the more religious family.[7]

Malcolm,

One of my friends who is not very sympathetic to the Christian faith says he has read that there is accumulating evidence for the God gene. He believes this shows we are religious because our genes have made us that way. Other people, and he would say he is one of those, are not religious because they do not have the God gene.

Ben,

I can guess where your friend heard about the so-called God gene. There have been media reports about this in some of the leading newspapers in the U.S. You only have to claim to show a genetic link between either sex or religion and you can guarantee wide media coverage. And that is just what happened with the report of possible links between genes and belief in God.

New York science journalist John Horgan, noting how some scientific discoveries are widely reported while others are not, wrote:

> As a journalist, I also understand all too well the media's fondness for discoveries of a gene for [fill in the blank]. We science reporters occupy a humble niche in the vast news and entertainment industry; even someone as experienced and talented as Jeffrey Kluger, who wrote the "God gene" story for *Time*, must compete fiercely for editors' and readers' attention. Discoveries of a "gay gene" or "God gene" are classic examples of what science writers call "gee-whiz" stories; the science is easy to understand, and its philosophical and social implications are titillating. Call it "gene-whiz" science.[8]

Horgan said, "The article left me pondering a different question: Given the track record of behavioral geneticists in general, and Dean Hamer in particular, why does anyone still take their claims seriously?" Horgan was referring to some of Hamer's earlier high-profile claims. So what did Hamer do, and what did he claim?

In 1993 Dean Hamer, with four colleagues, had claimed in *Science* that their study of forty pairs of gay brothers had turned up genetic markers in chromosome X associated with homosexuality. However, as Horgan noted, "Soon two other studies, involving more subjects than Hamer had used, found no evidence linking a gene in chromosome X to male homosexuality. Compared to Hamer's original claim, those contradictory reports received virtually no media coverage."

A paper appeared in mid-2011 with the title *The Behavior Genetics of Religiousness.* One of the authors, Matt McGue, is a past president of the Behavior Genetics Association and currently research professor at the Institute of Public Health at Southern Denmark University. In an introductory overview to all the papers in this journal issue on Genetics and Religion, Professor Elving Anderson, foreshadowing this paper, notes that, "Religiousness clearly is affected by genetic factors, but it is a complicated trait and the nature of the genetic influence is complex." Just how complicated is spelled out by Laura Koenig and Matt McGue in their paper.[9]

Following the lead given by Lindon Eaves, they note that two main ways of researching these issues are first, the twin study approach, and second, the adoption study approach, as well as additional evidence coming from the study of reared-apart twins.

The authors of this paper acknowledge at once that the whole concept of the measurement of religiousness is far from straightforward. They write,

"Religiousness, or the tendency to believe in a higher power and to act in ways consistent with that belief, is clearly a multi-faceted construct that spans attitudes, beliefs, practices and values. It is consequently not surprising that there is a plethora of ways of measuring religiousness, emphasizing anything from attendance at religious services and knowledge of specific religious dogma all the way through to spirituality and mysticism."

So what do they conclude from studies of religiousness based on adoption and reared-apart twins? First that "in childhood and adolescence, familial resemblance to religiousness is due predominantly to shared environmental factors, as socialization researchers predicted." However, they also note that "as we get older our experiences are increasingly a function of the choices we make, and these choices likely reflect underlying and, in part, genetically influenced dispositions, abilities and interests. The results here summarized indicate that religiousness follows this characteristic pattern. The choices we make regarding our religious attitudes, behaviors, and beliefs will not be independent of our dispositions and abilities, and thus will also be genetically influenced."

Their abstract sums it up nicely: "It is concluded that familial resemblance for religiousness is due largely to shared environmental factors in childhood and adolescence, but to genetic factors in adulthood. Additional evidence shows that there is a genetic correlation between religiousness and antisocial and altruistic behavior. Claims for the discovery of a 'God gene' are premature and unlikely, as any genetic influence is likely to represent the aggregate effect of many genetic factors." And with the dramatic claim by Dean Hamer that I mentioned above in mind, let me just give you the last sentence of their full paper: "There is no God gene."

Well I think that is a timely reminder that in assessing the results of any scientific research—especially when, for whatever reason, it hits the media headlines—we should do our best to be open-minded but be very careful not to be empty-minded. We can look forward to tremendous benefits to human well-being from genetic research reported in peer-reviewed journals, but we should be very cautious about knee-jerk reactions to headline-hitting claims of genetic links with emotionally charged issues such as sex and religion. It is clear that much research suggests that complex traits are the products of many genes, each having small effects.

5

Have Benjamin Libet's Experiments Exploded the Free-Will Myth?

Malcolm,

One of my friends, who is majoring in neuroscience, said that a very important paper was published in 1983 by a man named Benjamin Libet, who demonstrated that the conscious decision to make a movement came after the movement had been started. My friend said there had been several replications of Libet's experiment confirming his major findings. Doesn't that mean that any claim to decide to do this or do that is an illusion? That I'm merely reporting what my brain is already doing or has already done?

Ben,

Yes. Benjamin Libet and his colleagues studied the timing of events in the brain and their relation to mental phenomena. They devised ways of comparing the times at which events occur in the brain with those at which mental intentions were reported. Let me give you a bit of relevant background and an example of what they did.

Some time ago it was shown that electrodes attached to the head can record what is called a "slow negative potential shift" that occurs while someone is expecting a signal to which he will respond by making a movement. Around the same time, a related but rather more interesting discovery was that a similar kind of "readiness potential" occurs before a person makes a voluntary action. Libet and his collaborators showed that this readiness potential change in the brain takes place as much as half a second before a subject mentally decides that he intends to make a movement.[1]

They asked volunteers to sit and watch a television screen on which a spot was going around in circles in a clockwise direction at a rate of one revolution every two and a half seconds. The participants were asked to decide of their own free will to bend a finger and also to note the position of the spot on the screen at the moment they made their freely chosen decision. At the same time, using an electrode that the experimenter had attached to the subject's head, it was possible to record the "readiness potential" in the subject's brain. They found that these "readiness potential" changes began an average 350 milliseconds *before* the subject reported that he or she wanted or intended to act. Moreover, this was long before the time of actual movement of the finger, which was also detected by electrodes attached to it. It seemed therefore that this readiness potential arises from activities of neurons in what is known as the premotor area of the cortex. There are probably activities occurring in other parts of the brain at still earlier times before such an intended action.

The importance of Libet's work was that he showed that the brain seems to be at work before a person's conscious intention to act. Let me quote what he said in one of his publications: "Cerebral initiation even of a spontaneous voluntary act of the [kind] studied here can and usually does begin *unconsciously*. . . . The brain 'decides' to initiate or, at least, to prepare to initiate the act before there was any reportable subjective awareness that such a decision has taken place."[2]

The publication of these studies has led to a whole series of further ones, continuing still today. Perhaps not surprisingly these results were widely discussed by philosophers of mind and moral philosophers.

Malcolm,

I'm curious to know more about what has happened in the last thirty years since Libet reported his first experiments. Can you point me to a relatively recent paper that will help me get a better idea of what further experiments have discovered and how researchers are interpreting their data?

Ben,

In order to do my best to be up to date, I consulted a friend who is one of America's leading neurophysiologists. I asked him a bit about the state of play with regard to the interpretation of Libet's experiments, and to point me to a current paper dealing with these issues. He suggested a paper published a couple of years ago by Mark Hallett, Chief of the Human Motor Control Section at the National Institute of Neurological Disorders and Stroke in Bethesda, Maryland, and his colleagues.[3]

The paper is called, "The Timing of the Conscious Intention to Move." The opening sentence of the abstract of the paper reads, "The foundation of modern neuroscience and psychology about intention to action was laid by B. Libet." (So your friend was right on the ball when he shared with you his questions about wider implications of Libet's work.) Their methods have been criticized because they depended so much on self-reported timing by the participants and on subjective memory. The interpretation has been widely debated and, according to these authors, there is no general consensus as yet. (That has not prevented whole conferences of philosophers from meeting to discuss their implications for human free will!)

In their studies, Mark Hallett and his colleagues found that the mean time of the conscious intention to move was 1.42 seconds before movement. (This was estimated based on the subject's own real-time decision on whether or not there was a thought to move when a tone occurred.) They believe that their results solved some of the problems of the conventional methods of Libet's original studies and helped to give a clearer answer to some of the continuing controversies. They concluded, "The difference between the conventional result and our results suggests that the perception of intention rises through multiple levels of awareness starting just after the brain initiates movement."[4]

My neurophysiologist friend tells me that he and his fellow neurophysiologists discussed this paper in their journal club and that two things came out of their discussions. First, they noticed that there is a lot of subject-to-subject variation in the relationship between conscious intention to move and the early "readiness potential." They noted that the estimated time of the intention to move actually preceded or was somewhat tenuously linked with the early readiness potential of five of the fifteen subjects in the experiment. *That is a worryingly large proportion.* Second, they reanalyzed the data using a different technique and decided that the analysis given in Hallett's paper (one of the replications of Libet's experiments that I mentioned) had the effect of systematically biasing the majority of the measurements of the conscious intention to move toward later times, and at the same time biasing the early readiness potential to earlier times.

In the end, they were skeptical about the extent to which Hallett's paper did in fact support Libet's. They thought that a fairer analysis will probably show that the time of the conscious intention to move is not significantly different from the onset time of the readiness potential, and that is a very different interpretation from that advanced in the Libet paper. I should add that these neurophysiologists liked Hallet's experiment very much but were skeptical about the claimed result.

And that is how things stood until a paper appeared that seemed to call for a fresh look at what the so-called dependent variable in the Libet experiments was actually measuring. This was a paper by Jeff Miller and his colleagues at the University of Otago titled "Effects of Clock Monitoring on Electroencephalographic Activity: Is Unconscious Movement Initiation an Artifact of the Clock?"[5]

In this most recent study the researchers pointed out that the conclusion that the brain starts preparing to move before people consciously decide to move depends critically on the claim that the observed EEG activity specifically represents movement preparation. They point out that if the negative shift emerges from some brain processes other than movement preparation, then its appearance before the conscious decision to move does not support the claim that movement preparation begins unconsciously, which was Libet's claim.

The researchers carried out two experiments. In the first they examined participants' average EEG activity prior to a spontaneous key press movement; in the second experiment they measured EEG activity prior to a tone that was a stimulus for a pitch judgment task. They compared the condition in which participants monitored a clock to report the time at which they became conscious of a particular event—that is, the decision to move—in experiment 1 with the answer in experiment 2, the condition in which participants did not monitor a clock. This clock procedure had previously been used to estimate the time at which people become conscious of their decisions to move, and early results suggested that some types of EEG activity associated with movement preparation begin before the conscious decision to move (Libet's finding). Miller and his colleagues point out that the previous investigators had not explicitly addressed the possibility that the clock itself may have a direct influence on the EEG activity thought to index movement preparation. Let me quote from their results: "Our results challenge the conclusion that intentional movements are initiated by subconscious motor area activity. By calling into question the connection between this motor area activity and movement initiation, this challenge seems to fit well with arguments that the intention to move is not generated by a single brain area but is a product of a recurrent frontal-parietal network."[6] They concluded the abstract of their paper: "The effects of clock monitoring on EEG activity could be responsible for previous reports that movement-related brain activity begins before participants have consciously decided to move."[7]

If their results hold up and their interpretation is accepted, then it will turn out that a lot of ink has been used, mainly by philosophers, grappling with the question of how our subjective feelings of acting freely can be defended. I think there is a lesson here. As scientists we work as hard as we can to ensure that any deductions made from our experimental results are the only ones possible, or at least the most plausible, before we rush to the defense of wider beliefs that a quick interpretation seems to imply.

I've told you this because I think it well illustrates the need for caution by those who are not specialized, trained experimenters in building up large theories on the basis of such experiments. I rather fear that this is what has happened, judging from the way in which, as I mentioned earlier, philosophers have really gone to town suggesting that the whole notion of free will has to be reexamined and, as some would claim, turned upside down, on the basis of Libet's experiments and those that have followed it. Nothing could be further from the truth if we listen to those who are actually working on these experiments and understand what the results do and do not show.

I think we need to pause and ask whether experiments such as Libet's that studied the timing of a morally neutral, simple decision, such as bending a finger, and its relation to brain processes tells us anything useful about moral decision making. What I'm saying is that there is a fundamental problem with Libet's studies in the sense that they don't really have any obvious relevance for the question of free will and moral responsibility. Although Libet's subjects could freely choose the exact moment to move the wrist, they could not choose one action from a certain morally different action. The overwhelming phenomenological evidence from our daily lives is that we make conscious, voluntary decisions that influence the activity of our brains and bodies over minutes, days and years, not milliseconds, and that these decisions bring real-world consequences.

There is another feature of the artificiality of the Libet-type experiments that has been nicely brought out by a study just published by a group of Italian scientists. They make the point that you need to take into account the possible effects of someone's privately held belief systems when taking part in something as seemingly simple as responding in a Libet-type experiment. They asked the question, What would happen if people started to disbelieve in free will? They noted that undermining free-will beliefs had already been shown to influence social behavior. In their study they asked the question of whether undermining beliefs in free will might affect the brain correlates of voluntary motor preparation of the kind studied by Libet. One of the two groups in their experiment, called the "no-free-will" group, read a passage from a famous book claiming that scientists now recognize that free will is an illusion. The other group, the control group, read a passage on consciousness from the same book that did not mention free will. In order to ensure that the participants read the material carefully, they were told that a comprehension test would be given at the end of the experiment. What they found was that the readiness potential that they measured was reduced in those individuals who were induced to disbelieve in free will. This they said was evident more than one second before participants consciously decided to move, a finding that suggests that the manipulation influenced intentional actions at preconscious stages.

Malcolm,

What did Mark Hallet have to say about any possible implications of these experiments and whether his own attempts to replicate them had any relevance to wider issues about free will?

Ben,

At the time of his own research, Hallet noted that we all have a common perception that we enjoy free will to, for example, voluntarily choose to make our own movements. This, he said, is taken for granted. He also noted that discussions of free will are frequently mixed up with discussions of consciousness, which points to an equally, if not more, difficult problem that even philosophers have now begun to call "the hard problem."

On consciousness and free will, Hallet notes that over the centuries there have been two general views. On the one hand, a dualist view claims that the brain and mind are separate, that scientists simply study the brain, and that consciousness is, as he puts it, "a separate feature of the mind." On the other hand is Hallett's own view, which claims that the evidence does not support the dualist understanding. His view is what he and others label "monism." This is the view that mind, as he puts it, is a product of brain.[8] As you know, my own view is a qualified monist view. It is more accurate to say that the mind and brain are both *aspects* of a single reality, so my view is one of dual-aspect monism.

Hallett thinks his view has wider implications. So at the end of his paper he writes about its "implications for morality and the law." He asks, "If there is no free will as a driving force, are persons responsible for their behavior?" He believes this is only a difficult question to the dualist. I agree. However, I think Hallett himself is not as careful as he might have been when he writes: "A person's brain is clearly fully responsible, and always responsible, for the person's behavior."[9] I think I know what he means, but it is people who have responsibilities, not brains. That of course applies in what I would call normal circumstances.

Malcolm,

What do you mean by normal circumstances? Do you mean that some of us have brains that make free will possible and some of us don't? That seems unfair. And how do we know if and when we are responsible for our actions?

Ben,

I should have guessed you might ask that. Both Libet's and Hallett's experiments involved making voluntary movements, and it was the result of those studies that prompted their discussions of free will. And it was those studies that prompted me to say "in normal conditions." However, it is worth remembering that there are occasions when involuntary movements occur in neurological patients.

In one such condition, a patient would reach out and do things with one of her hands, over which she felt she had no control, and often did things that embarrassed her. A patient's family, for example, told the neurologist how the lady, out of the blue and much to her dismay, reached out with her left hand while at a restaurant, took some leftover fish bones and put them in her mouth. On another occasion, to her embarrassment, she reached out and grabbed her brother's ice cream. She claimed that her left hand "had a mind of its own" and often did whatever pleased it. What happens here is that people experience a conflict between their declared will and the action of one of their hands.

Some years ago, when I was still actively researching the functions of the corpus callosum, I was asked to see a lady who had part of her corpus callosum cut in order to remove a tumor. In my preliminary conversations with her, she recalled the embarrassment of tying a scarf around her neck with one hand, only to have the other hand reach out and start taking it off. Her husband would also tell her that at breakfast she would pick up the spoon to eat her cereal with one hand, and her other hand would reach across and take it out of her first hand. Understandably, she found it very distressing.

Another condition was portrayed in the Peter Sellers film *Dr. Strangelove,* which was based on the novel *Red Alert.* A German-American nuclear scientist, played by Peter Sellers, constantly had to grab his right arm to stop it from making a Nazi salute! Today what used to be known as the anarchic hand syndrome is now known as the Dr. Strangelove syndrome in the popular scientific press.

I won't trouble you with details of what goes wrong anatomically in the anarchic hand syndrome. There was a time when it was thought to be, as in the case of the person I saw, due to an interhemispheric disconnection. That may be true in some cases, but nowadays the consensus is that it occurs more commonly from damage in an area of the brain known as the supplementary motor area. So there is continuing debate among neurologists and neuropsychologists about the relative parts played, whether by discrete lesions in the corpus callosum and/or damage to the mesial frontal lobe. The point is that there are neurological conditions of which we are aware and of which we can say with some confidence that the damage to specific areas of the brain makes it difficult to control involuntary movements of the hands. I suppose you could call this not lack of free will but lack of "free won't." Mark Hallett describes some of his own experiments as studies of "free won't."

I think it is noteworthy that he usefully reminds us, "Behavior, like all other elements of a person, is a product of that person's genetics and experience. A person's behavior should be able to be influenced by specific environmental interventions, such as reward and punishment."[10]

My mention of the corpus callosum reminds me that very recently one of the leading researchers for forty years into the functions of the corpus callosum, Michael Gazzaniga, has shared his considered views on a range of wider issues related to neuroscience, including free will. He has just published a book titled *Who's in Charge: Free Will and the Science of the Brain*, based on his lifetime of experience in cutting-edge neuroscience, and his views are worth heeding.

Gazzaniga is keen to expose some of the errors of unthinking reductionism. So he says that just as you cannot explain traffic patterns by studying car parts, neuroscience must abandon its tendency to reduce macrolevel phenomena like free will to microlevel explanations. In an interview, when he was asked about his views on determinism, he commented:

> What I mean is that determinism at one level, suggests that we are kind of just along for the ride. It's all done for us. Neuroscience is constantly unearthing mechanisms for understanding behavior and cognition. Neuroscience provides more and more evidence for a mechanistic view of the human mind. A lot of people find that bleak and don't like it. I say: it's not bleak, it's just the way the machine works. The fundamental value that we all hold in human culture is that we want people to be held personally responsible for their actions. Once you learn how the machine works, does that mean that you are not responsible for your actions because your behavior may be determined? No, I don't think it means that at all. The idea of social responsibility arises out of a social group. It's in the laws of interaction between people and you

> don't look for it in the brain any more than you'd look for the answer to understand traffic by understanding car parts. It's another level of organization that you are trying to understand.[11]

Later he was asked, "Am I deluding myself when I think that I'm making independent responsible choices?" His answer was no. "What you're doing is that your brain is building a belief or plan of action that you think is wise for you. It exists in your cognitive system and you want to attend to it. Now the question is whether you do. How many do you attend to and how many do you not? It's really personal for you, but there is accountability in your own cognitive 'I think those things are real.' What you're saying is that you can have this whole social contract model within your head, right?"[12]

And that leads to another important point made by Gazzaniga. When asked, "Can brain science tell exactly where automatic processes end and self-directed 'responsible' ones [begin]?" he responded, "Not now and not likely ever. . . . Social constructs like good judgment and free will are even further removed, and trying to define them in terms of biological processes is, in the end, a fool's game."[13]

And that leads immediately into one of the most rapidly expanding areas of neuroscience—social neuroscience. But first, I want to tell you about a recent bit of news regarding Benjamin Libet's experiments. A report published in the Proceedings of the National Academy of Sciences in America in August 2012 has come up with another challenge to the widely held interpretation of Libet's experiments. Its author, Aaron Schurger of the National Institutes of Health and Medical Research in Saclay in France, notes, "Even people who have been critical of Libet's work, by and large, haven't challenged that assumption"—namely, that the EEG recordings showing a signal in the brain 550 milliseconds earlier than a decision to act was made were interpreted as suggesting that "the brain prepares to act well before we are conscious of the urge to move."[14]

As I mentioned previously, there was an earlier challenge by New Zealanders Judy Treverne and Jeff Milten. Now here is another. Schurger presents the evidence from their EEG studies and says, "We have argued that what looks like a pre-conscious decision process *may not in fact reflect a decision at all*. It only looks that way because of the nature of spontaneous brain activity." They conclude, "If we are correct, then the Libet experiment does not count as evidence against the possibility of conscious will."[15]

Anil Seth, a cognitive neuroscientist at the University of Sussex in the UK, commenting on these experiments and their interpretation, notes, "The new model is 'opening the door toward a richer understanding of the neural basis of the conscious experience of volition.'"[16] And this "conscious experience of volition" is a well-nigh universal human experience and should remind us that there is nothing remotely scientific about denying or rejecting this universal experience on the basis of Libet's experiments. So watch this space!

6

But Is It All in the Brain?

The Emergence of Social Neuroscience

Malcolm,

I'm currently having a course of lectures on social psychology. It seems to me that the people who have reported research on the link between mind and brain have left out the significant personal side of what it means to be human. Aren't we social creatures? Our whole lives are lived interacting with other people. Do you think there has been an overemphasis on brain processes, at the expense of considering our social interactions?

Ben,

Your question brings to mind a wise comment I read recently by a leading philosopher. He said it is not good enough to "tell the truth"; we must "tell the whole truth." You are quite correct that an overconcentration on the single individual in neuropsychological research leaves out an important component of human behavior. I imagine it will sound a bit defensive on my part, but I think I would say first of all that the problems we face in trying to understand the links between mind and brain are in themselves so challenging that, following normal scientific procedures, we begin by reducing the uncontrolled variables as much as possible, and even then it is not always easy to interpret the data unambiguously. So we begin by studying individuals in laboratory settings. Having said that, you will be pleased to hear that, as I mentioned earlier, one of the fastest developing areas today in neuroscience is social neuroscience.

A 2004 book was titled *The Neuroscience of Social Interaction*,[1] and a 2005 book was titled simply *Social Neuroscience.*[2] Both books are good examples of contemporary social neuroscience research. The contents of the 2005 book give you the flavor of how neuroscientists are making a start at understanding the importance in brain research of social factors and social interactions, and how these are dependent upon and, in turn, influence brain processes.

I think it is significant that in the preface to the 2005 book, we read, "Attempting to canvas the full scope of social neuroscience would deprive the reader of the rich depth and coherence that can come from multilevel analyses of some of the most fascinating questions humanity has asked about itself and the human mind."[3] This should alert you at once to the fact that the contributors are fully aware and acknowledge that analysis of human behavior at any one level must be supplemented by analyses at other levels to gain a meaningful and coherent picture. To analyze behavior only at one level may tell the truth about what is happening at that level, but it will certainly not tell the whole truth about human behavior.

As if to underline the need never to forget that as biological beings we live our lives in social contexts, I see that there is a symposium planned for the May meeting of the APS. The advance notice for this meeting reads, "Nature versus nurture? Not anymore! In today's psychological science they are on the same team. Research reveals the interdependence among biological systems and social contexts. Environmental and interpersonal factors influence the expression of genes, the development of the brain, and the growth of the individual from the beginnings of life."

Although the field has only really taken off in recent years, there have been clues to how it might develop for more than a century. A classic case, which you know all about, was the occasion when Phineas Gage accidentally damaged the frontal lobes of his brain and from then on showed dramatic changes in his social behavior and in his personality. More recent research has confirmed that the superior temporal sulcus is involved in specifying the social and emotional relevance of some forms of social behavior. Since then others have written at length on this. For example, Antonio Damasio and his colleagues have demonstrated how specific parts of the brain are involved in social perception and cognition and decision making. The ongoing debates among leaders in the field about the specific contribution to social cognition made by various nuclei in the brain shows where research is moving today in this rapidly developing field.

Malcolm,

Yes, I have heard about Phineas Gage but, so far, not much about more recent developments. Can you tell me more?

Ben,

Yes, one of the volumes I mentioned is a good place to start. Conscious of the fact that there is a sporadic history of investigations of patients with brain damage, as well as controlled studies using animals as experimental subjects, it is not surprising that the editors of *Social Neuroscience* comment that, "In sum, the question is not whether, but where and how activity in the brain serves a social process that has the potential to inform theory in the social and brain sciences."[4]

A few examples from the published papers brought together in this book illustrate what the editors had in mind. One of the possible ways of monitoring what's happening in the brain, in a noninvasive way, is by using event-related functional magnetic resonance imaging, or fMRI, which makes possible measuring neural activity when people are doing particular tasks. I have mentioned this before, but perhaps I ought to explain more about how it works. Only if you know that can you judge how accurate it is and how open to misinterpretation some of the results are that appear in the media.

FMRI works by measuring the oxygen consumed by active neurons in the brain. When neurons are active they take oxygen from the bloodstream, and a magnetic property of the hemoglobin changes. The powerful magnets in the machine line up the hemoglobin molecules and then cause them to spin and emit energy. By measuring this energy the machine tells which areas are more active when, for example, we think or feel or plan specific actions. As a technique it is extremely helpful and very important. However, a bit like phrenology in the past—when people felt the bumps on the outside of people's heads to understand how their minds worked—there is a danger that the results of fMRI studies can be abused to the extent that they become a sort of modern phrenology. That would be deeply regrettable since they have tremendous potential for current research in neuroscience.

In one instance, using these techniques, the experimenters asked the subjects to look at briefly presented noun and adjective pairs of words. The participants had to press one button if the adjective could be true of the noun, and another button if it could not. Nouns were either the names of persons or the names of objects of clothing or of fruit. Some of the adjectives could describe a person—for example, energetic or fickle or nervous—but wouldn't be relevant to any of the objects (items of clothing or fruit). The remaining half of the adjectives could describe one of the class of objects but not persons. Some of the adjectives, while appropriate to describing one of the class of the objects, were not appropriate to the other. So a piece of clothing could be "patched" or "threadbare" or a piece of fruit could be "seedless" or "sun-dried." What they found was that the results suggested distinct networks in the brain subserving the representation of semantic knowledge, some about people and some about objects. People, of course, are involved in social interactions and objects are not, so the results showed that there are systems selectively mobilized where social factors are involved.

I'm sure *Social Neuroscience* will be in your library, so I won't list too many more examples. But here is one more. I think most people agree that successful social interaction depends, in part at least, on how we appraise other people from their faces. One aspect of this is whether we judge other people to be trustworthy. Using fMRI, researchers studied the neural basis for making judgments of trustworthiness of faces. They showed that a part of the brain called the right superior temporal sulcus showed enhanced activity when judgments of trustworthiness were being made.

I think it is significant that in the final part of *Social Neuroscience* the editors wrote a brief essay under the title "Biological Does Not Mean Predetermined: Reciprocal Influences of Social and Biological Processes."[5] This I know you will recognize as taking us back to some of our earlier discussions about whether, if you can identify a biological basis for some aspect of our behavior, it means we have no freedom of action. In the final paragraph of this short essay, the editors wrote,

> In sum, all human behavior, at some level, is biological, but this is not to say that biological representation yields a simple, singular, or satisfactory explanation of complex behaviors, or that molecular forms of representation provide *the only or best level of analysis for understanding human behavior.* Molar constructs such as those developed by social psychologists provide a means of understanding highly complex activity without needing to specify each individual action of the simplest components, thereby providing an efficient means of describing the behavior of a complex system. Social and biological approaches to human behavior have traditionally been contrasted, as if the two were antagonistic or mutually exclusive. The readings in this book *demonstrate the fallacy of this reasoning and suggest that the mechanisms underlying mind and behavior may not be fully explicable by a biological or a social approach alone but, rather, that a multilevel integrative analysis may be required.*[6]

In short, an *exhaustive* explanation at one chosen level of investigation cannot, without further justification, claim to be the only and *exclusive* explanation necessary to a full understanding of what is being studied.

Malcolm,

Some of the quotes you gave me reminded me of something I've wanted to ask about for a while. Whatever has happened to consciousness in the hands of psychologists? Surely that is the most real and obvious feature of our lives?

Ben,

Your question is spot-on. I think the general public shares your puzzlement about why psychologists have for many years talked so little about consciousness. For more than half a century in the writings of the majority of psychologists, consciousness seemed to drop from sight. Not so before that, when under Sigmund Freud's influence, discussions of consciousness and the unconscious occupied center stage.

Fifty years ago, when behaviorism, championed by B. F. Skinner, was at its height in North America, talk about the mind or consciousness was considered to be "too mentalistic, too subjective, too shifty." One of the leading experimental psychologists of the time who did not share Skinner's views,

Professor George Miller, commented, "You're supposed to get at the mind through the eye, the ear, the nose and throat if you are a real psychologist."

Illustrating what was happening at that time, if you were to look back at the standard reference work in experimental psychology that I used as a student in 1951—the *Handbook of Experimental Psychology*, edited by S. S. Stevens[7]—you would find that of its 1362 pages only 27 were devoted to anything like mind talk, and that was in a short chapter on cognitive processes. Today, as you well know, when cognitive psychology is so dominant and cognitive neuroscience so productive, such a relegation of mind to something approaching insignificance is very difficult to understand.

Today it looks as if consciousness is being regained. There are many books and journal papers published today on consciousness, and the relation of mind and brain. But you may ask, Are consciousness and mind the same thing? Some people say they are. Others argue that mind is not synonymous with consciousness. They say that while mind enables human beings, and no doubt other creatures, to handle the vast amount of information bombarding them at all times, to reflect on that information and then to go beyond it to anticipate, to plan and to act, consciousness is seen as another instrument of mind; there is a lot more than mind to consciousness. Thus, we can say with justification that *mind* refers to a set of high-level cognitive processes and that consciousness emerges from these processes—but consciousness is not necessary for most of these processes.

As we discussed some time back, in the past two decades psychologists have become increasingly interested in the study of top-down effects. One key feature of these studies has been their demonstration that what, at any moment, we are focusing our thoughts on, selectively mobilizes specific brain regions and systems. Perhaps top-down effects are the beginnings of evidence for the elusive scientific foundations we are seeking when we want to study consciousness in action.

It is not only in neuropsychology where consciousness has come under the scientific microscope. Other areas of psychology where developments on the nature of consciousness is having significant impacts are social psychology and personality psychology. For example, David Myers, a social psychologist, has written at length about the two ways of knowing, the automatic (unconscious) and controlled (conscious). Myers has shown that research in this area demands that we take a fresh, critical look at social intuitions and clinical intuitions.[8]

Another example is in the area of personality psychology where, for example, Robert Emmons has explored current models of conscious and unconscious influences in the field of personality research, showing how personal striving is a product of the joint operation of the two systems.[9] In their different ways, approaches such as these reopen a question that is addressed at length in a chapter by Baumeister, Masicampo and Vohs titled "Do Conscious Thoughts Cause Behavior?" just published in the *Annual Review of Psychology* in 2011.[10] Have a look at it when it comes into your university library.

7

But What About the Soul?

Malcolm,

When we talked a while ago about the mind-brain relationship, you repeatedly referred to our "psychobiological unity." I think I know what you mean, but since it seems to be so central to much of what you have written, can you tell me more? First, is it your personal view only, or is it shared by your fellow scientists? And second, does it have implications for a scriptural understanding of humanity? I've always understood that a dominant biblical theme is that we are unique because, according to Genesis, we alone possess an immortal soul.

Ben,

Your first question is, in a way, the easier and more straightforward. Although there have been some very distinguished scientists, including Nobel laureates, who believed in a separate immortal soul, they are in a very small minority. The majority, as far as I can judge, would share the view expressed recently by Chris Frith, one of today's leading cognitive neuroscientists, when he wrote that he "wanted to combat the persistent dualist denial that there is any relation between the physical world of the brain and the mental world of the mind."[1] The late Sir John Eccles, a neurophysiologist and Nobel laureate, was fully aware of the tight links between mind and brain. He nevertheless believed that we possess an immaterial, immortal soul that can and does interact with our bodies and brains. Such a view has a long and distinguished record in the history of the Christian church.

For two millennia a pervasive theme of dogmatic and systematic theology, when focusing on theological anthropology and the doctrine of humanity and considering human uniqueness, emphasized that humankind alone is created "in the divine image" or "in the image of God." This refers, of course, to Genesis 1:27: "God created man in his own image, in the image of God he created him." On this view, a straightforward answer to the question of what makes us human and distinguishes us from the rest of creation was that, since God is a spiritual being, he endowed us also with spirituality, giving us an immortal soul. There are, however, other ways of understanding this text and what it teaches about what makes us unique.

James Barr, for example, helpfully identifies five ways in which the image of God has been interpreted in the past. First, we possess an immortal soul. Second, we alone can reason (argued by Augustine and Aquinas and accepted by Luther and many of the Reformers). A third was based on our physical distinctiveness, bipedalism and so on. Fourth is what Barr labels "functionality," or our calling to have dominion over the world. In this sense the image of God is not what we are but what we are called to do. Fifth is our capacity for a relationship with God and with other creatures, an idea emphasized by Karl Barth, for whom the image of God becomes not just an ability for relationship, but the relationship itself: a relationship with God and with each other, most clearly exemplified in Jesus, who alone is fully the image of God.[2]

You are correct: Christians in the past made regular appeal to our possessing a soul as part of the proof that humans are not mere animals. Tertullian, for example, had no doubt that "without the soul, we are nothing." On this view the possession of the soul is the foundation of our human dignity and confers sacredness on human life. The notion of the existence of a nonphysical soul, which is distinct and separate from the body, has also been regarded as the means by which humans can cross over the bridge between this life and the next. Traditional Christian thought has seen the body as frail and finite, whereas the soul is immortal.

In trying to answer your questions briefly I face the danger of falling into a trap that others have fallen into of pretending that there are simple answers to profound questions. However, if I try to follow what linguistic and biblical scholars are currently saying, they recognize a gross oversimplification in the long-standing and pervasive view that there was a dichotomy between Hebrew thought (which affirmed some form of psychosomatic unity, what others called psychobiological unity) and Greek thought (which affirmed some form of dualism—a separate soul and body). That is because Greek thought was much more varied on the nature of the soul than you would suppose from readings focused solely on Plato would suggest. As one scholar in this area put it, "There was no singular conception of the soul among the Greeks, and the body-soul relationship was variously assessed among philosophers and physicians in the Hellenistic period."[3]

The relationship between Hellenism and Judaism in the centuries after the successes of Alexander the Great in the near East in the last half of the fourth century before Christ was a complex one. The result was that the environment within which the New Testament took shape provided for the presence of a variety of views both within Roman Hellenism and within Hellenistic Judaism.

We need to remember that for centuries the words *soul* and *mind* were used interchangeably. However, statements such as "in philosophical and Christian thinking, the attributes of the soul and the mind were seen as essentially the same" are oversimplifications. Within the Christian context the obvious proof text for the existence and the importance of the soul is found right at the beginning of the Bible in Genesis 2:7 where, in the familiar King James version, we read, "And the LORD God formed man of the dust of the ground, and breathed into his nostrils the breath of life; and man became a living soul." The traditional understanding of this is that God took physical material—the dust—and by a unique act of special creation gave to it a nonmaterial spiritual essence. This was "the breath of life" by which humanity became a creature possessing a soul or a spiritual nature. Thus, on this view, it is this soul that departs the body at death, lives in a spiritual domain, and is reunited with the body at the resurrection of the dead on the last day. Hence, for many, the vital need to defend the status of the soul in defining our humanity. However, such a view is widely challenged today by biblical scholars who see a defining feature of what makes us special as arising first and foremost from our calling, also in the Genesis narrative, to enter into the personal relationship offered to us by our Creator.

One of today's leading biblical scholars and an expert on hermeneutics places the same emphasis when he writes, "'Image of God' denotes above all the calling to represent God. Only derivatively and secondarily does it imply bearing a God-like set of dispositions or qualities."[4] Another scholar, Tom Wright, wrote to me in correspondence about this: "I have been arguing for some time: that 'image of God' was not, in Genesis 1, intended to refer to some characteristic or special ability or trait of humans but rather to a vocation. . . . The vocation in question is that humans were designed by the creator to have a special role in his governance of the world. Eventually it comes round to using the 'royal priesthood' language which I think is absolutely central."[5]

Malcolm,

From what you have just written, I take it that you share the views of biblical scholars such as Anthony Thiselton and Tom Wright? Their views are not the ones that I and many of my Christian friends have grown up with. Are you suggesting that I need to rethink them?

Ben,

Yes, I suppose I am. I recognize, of course, that this is a big topic widely debated among biblical scholars and theologians and that there are different views. I can point you to some sources where you can listen to biblical scholars digging into the detailed exegesis of some of the words used in the key passages in Genesis that you referred to. Like you, I am not a Hebrew scholar, so I am dependent on their expertise. Reading what they have to say makes clear certain things that I find helpful.

The notion of "dust" in Old Testament texts is primarily associated with fragility and mortality. In this sense the fact that we are dust underlines our fragility and mortality, something already evident in what has been written about the animals earlier in Genesis. More importantly for our present discussion is what is meant by "the breath of life" in the Genesis passage. Traditionally, and until relatively recently, this has been interpreted in a way that suggests that life is given to Adam in an act of divine special creation. The sense I get now is that biblical scholars conclude that closer examination of all the relevant evidence, including the Genesis passages, makes it clear that "the breath of life" does not distinguish Adam from the animals, rather it binds him to them. They point out that precisely the same words used when referring to the creation of the animals are used in this passage referring to humankind. There are no grounds for claiming that it denotes the creation of an immaterial entity within human nature that sets humans apart from the animals.

The appeal to this key passage in Genesis 2:7, and what it teaches about human nature, comes right at the end of the creation story. It declares that God breathed into the dust and formed Adam. It was thus by this "breath of life," according to the King James Version, that Adam became "a living soul." It is interesting how different English versions reflect the different presuppositions the translators brought to this passage.

In the King James Version we have the word *soul,* reflecting the ancient equivalent in the Greek Old Testament of the *nefesh,* or soul. (Some writers render this *nephesh;* others, as I have done here, as *nefesh.*) Most modern versions, however, translate it "a living being." One even translates it "and the man became a living person" (NLT). The question is, Does this text say something very important about the unique quality of human existence, about personhood, and is this to be expressed by the term *soul,* or is it saying something about the animation of the inspired dust as it comes alive? If you really want to go into this, I warn you, there are almost eight hundred occurrences of the word *nefesh* in the Old Testament!

Malcolm,

I confess that I just don't have the time to research this term in the Old Testament, even if I wanted to. Would you be willing to quickly summarize for me the conclusions of scholars who have done this, particularly scholars who share our approach to Scripture?

Ben,

Your question is not of academic interest only. A paper has just been published in a medical journal with the title, "The Mortal Soul in Ancient Israel and Pauline Christianity: Ramifications for Modern Medicine."[6] I mention this, first, because if you read it you will find it gives a succinct answer to your question, and second, because it shows that the answers given to the questions you raise are relevant, not only for psychologists and neuroscientists, but also for the practice of medicine.

I am also happy to give you a summary of the views of a typical professor of Old Testament who teaches at a college in your own church tradition, on this question of how best to understand the soul. Professor Lawson Stone, at Asbury Theological Seminary in the U.S., makes a number of important points that I'm just going to quote for you:

1. Regarding what happened when "God breathed into Adam," he writes, "We are not to imagine Adam's reception of some intangible personal essence makes him human, distinct from the animals, and eligible for everlasting life. The *nefesh* here is not a possession, nor is it a component of Adam's nature, a 'part.' The pile of dust, upon being inspirited by divine breath actually became a living *nefesh.* The term 'living *nefesh*' then denotes the totality of Adam's being. Adam does not 'have' a *nefesh;* he is a 'living *nefesh.*'"
2. Stone then asks, What *is* a "living *nefesh*"? He says that the simplest answer is found in the immediate context. The term *living soul* appears four times in the preceding context and once shortly after. Thus in Genesis 1:21, 24, 30, the term refers simply and clearly to animals. In these passages the expression can be rendered "living creature." And later he goes on to say, referring to the animals, "that each one, like him, is a living '*nefesh*' and this clearly underscores the conclusion that a living '*nefesh*' is not a being separate from the rest of creation because it possesses an intangible spiritual entity that determines its identity."
3. Stone continues, "The linking of *nefesh* to physical existence and not to transcendence, to an immortal inward essence of personhood, fits well with the Old Testament's overall disinterest in the afterlife. . . . To summarise: the term *nefesh* in Genesis 2 verse 7 refers not to a part of Adam's nature, nor to some possession such as a transcendent personal spiritual hypostasis termed a 'soul' that lives forever and distinguishes humanity from the animals. Rather, *nefesh hayyah* denotes Adam as a living creature like the animals created in Genesis 1 and 2. It underscores Adam's linkage with the animal creation, not his difference from it."[7]

I think it is also important to realize that the views expressed here by Lawson Stone are not new but have been in circulation in Christian circles for some time. A quarter of a century earlier, H. D. McDonald, another biblical scholar, endorsed these views and at the same time illustrated the varied meanings of *nefesh* in the Old Testament and showed how this links to *psyche* in the New Testament. He wrote,

> The Hebrew word for soul (*nefesh*), which occurs more than seven hundred times in the Old Testament, has the general meaning "possessing life." In this connection it can be used of animals (e.g., Gen. 1:20). Most of its many uses in the Psalms carry the connotation of "life-principle." It has a distinctively physical reference in numerous passages (e.g., Job 33:20) and a psychological reference (moral action) in others (e.g., Job 7:15). It is sometimes used to specify the individual person (e.g., Lev. 7:21) or the self (e.g., Judg. 16:16; Ps. 120:6). The Greek word *psyche* has in the New Testament the same general meaning as *nefesh* in the Old. Its occurrences in the epistles of Paul are variously translated in the Revised Standard Version: "human being" (Rom. 2:9); "person" (Rom. 13:1); "living being" (1 Cor. 15:45); "self" (1 Thess. 2:8); "life" (Rom. 11:3; 16:4; Phil. 2:30); "mind" (Phil. 1:27); and "heart" (Eph. 6:6). This diversity of usage conditions its general meaning. As the vital principle of individual life, the "soul" may refer to the concrete individual (Rom. 2:9) or to specific psychical elements which make up the person.[8]

I have quoted this detailed information with the biblical references because I know you like to check for yourself any of the claims that are made by such writers. I hope very much that just looking at this restricted number of biblical references will help to remind you that when you hear someone persuading you of a particular model of the human person from Scripture, remember that you need to be alert lest an oversimplification is being presented to you that does not have any clear biblical warrant.

Well, there you have it. I warned you that it might be a thought-provoking set of quotations to digest, but I think they're extremely important. And just to make it clear that I am not dependent only on the contributions of biblical scholars from what must seem to you like an earlier generation, may I suggest that you will find the very recent writings of Old Testament scholar Peter Enns helpful and illuminating on these same issues.[9] I would suggest that he further underlines and amplifies the contributions I quoted from scholars such as Lawson Stone.

Malcolm,

Thank you for that. It was helpful, illuminating and, as you said, rather thought-provoking. I'm wondering, though, about Christians from past centuries whose writings, it seems to me, the Christian church takes very seriously. In the views you've outlined for me, would their convictions and teachings about the soul be misleading, or even wrong, in light of today's biblical scholarship? But isn't it arrogant to think that our generation is the one to finally arrive at the truth?

Ben,

An understandable reaction. I think it's all too easy for us today, helped as we are by these diligent biblical scholars, to be smug about *our* understanding and how it supersedes that of our forebears. With the benefit of hindsight, I think we are all too ready to be overly and unfairly critical of our Christian forebears who, in their generation, and for good reasons, had no doubt that it was proper to interpret certain Scriptures in a way that is different from ours. Often it was a tendency, in a prescientific era, to interpret certain texts literally. For example, they believed

1. that the earth rests on pillars (1 Samuel 2:8 in the King James Version, but compare the New International Version [1984]: "For the foundations of the earth are the LORD's; upon them he has set the world");
2. that the earth does not move but stands still (1 Chronicles 16:30 in the King James Version, but the New International Version says, "The world is firmly established; it cannot be moved");
3. that the earth has ends and edges (Job 37:3 KJV; NIV reads, "sends it to the ends of the earth"); and
4. that the earth has four corners (Isaiah 11:12 KJV; NIV says, "from the four quarters of the earth"; also Revelation 7:1 KJV, or in NIV, "I saw four angels standing at the four corners of the earth").

Further, what pertains in the interpretation of Scripture passages in light of today's geological and astronomical knowledge also applies as we, in our generation, review some passages of Scripture in light of modern biology. For example,

1. bats are not birds (Leviticus 11:13-19; Deuteronomy 14:11-18);
2. camels do have cloven hooves (Leviticus 11:4);
3. turtles do not have voices (Song of Solomon 2:12 KJV); and
4. no four-legged animals fly (Leviticus 11:21), unless you include gliding foxes?

In each of these instances the contrast is clear between how scientific books and papers in astronomy, astrophysics, geology, zoology and botany write about the earth, the stars, the plants and the animals, and how Scripture refers to them. We are no longer tempted to see the scientific accounts as competitors with the biblical accounts. Nor do we seek to intermix them or to incorporate the one into the other; that way lies confusion and an unwitting abuse of Scripture. So in some ways we modern Christians have an advantage. We don't need to struggle to harmonize biblical and scientific descriptions from biology and astronomy. They are so self-evidently different in origin and purpose.

Malcolm,

Your points about the relevance of biblical knowledge are well taken. Now I'm curious to know whether, and in what ways, advances in scientific psychology may prompt us to pause as we read parts of the Bible talking about human nature and repeat interpretations of the Bible that we have grown up with. Should science control biblical interpretation? Or should biblical interpretation control science?

Ben,

Good questions. Let me extend what we were talking about to psychology and neuroscience and to current discussions about mind and the way it is used in contemporary cognitive psychology and neuropsychology. The way the mind is used in psychology and the way it is typically used and interpreted in Scripture are not the same, though there is occasional overlap, which can lead to confusion. Let me illustrate.

When the apostle Paul is writing to the Christians in Rome, he refers repeatedly to our sinful nature. In one of his commentaries on this, John Stott emphasizes that Romans 8 is, in his view, full of profound teaching about human nature. Yet anyone who reads it is at once aware that he's reading theology, not psychology, at least not psychology as it is understood today. Nevertheless, in a more general sense, Paul shares some profound psychological insights. Stott writes,

> Here Paul concentrates on the "mind", or (as we would say) "mindset", of those who are characterized by either *sarx* or *pneuma*. . . . Our mindset ex-

> presses our basic nature as Christians or non-Christians. . . . The meaning surely is not that people are like this because they think like this, although that is partly true, but that they think like this because they are like this. The expressions are descriptive. In both cases their nature determines their mindset. Moreover, since the flesh is our twisted human nature, its desires are all those things which pander to our ungodly self-centredness.[10]

John Stott later sums up this section of his commentary:

> To sum up, here are two categories of people (the unregenerate who are "in the flesh" and the regenerate who are "in the Spirit"), who have two perspectives or mindsets ("the mind of the flesh" and "the mind of the Spirit"), which lead to two patterns of conduct (living according to the flesh or the Spirit), and result in two spiritual states (death or life, enmity or peace). Thus our mind, where we set it and how we occupy it, plays a key role in both our present conduct and our final destiny.[11]

Note the repeated references here to human nature, to mind, to mindset ("mindset" is rather akin to what psychologists call "attitudes"), to the unregenerate and the regenerate. This all makes good sense to the Christian and is self-evidently not the language of scientific psychology, but nevertheless it is powerfully and penetratingly true. So the take-home message again is, watch your language and note carefully the context in which the word or words are being used, and in that way you'll be helped to avoid producing false conflicts and generating unnecessary problems.

Malcolm,

You mentioned how necessary it is not to read back into passages of the Bible the meaning of words like *mind* that we are so familiar with today. The example you gave from some of John Stott's writings was particularly helpful.

However, so far in your emails about understanding the soul, you have focused mostly on the early chapters of Genesis. As I read the Psalms, what I might call a "natural reading," it seems like the psalmist views the soul as a separate "thing." (For example, the psalmist repeatedly says, "my soul" does this or that.) How does that fit with what you've said about the word *soul* in Genesis? And can you tell me something more about how the word *soul* is used and understood in the New Testament?

Ben,

I have known you long enough now to realize that you are not going to let me off the hook easily. I think the best way I can answer your question about the way that the Psalms use the word *soul* is to refer you to an InterVarsity Press book that I know you have: the commentary on the Psalms by Derek Kidner. I think he is helpful on what you call the "natural reading" of the Psalms—namely, that the soul is a separate thing. I would like to suggest that, following accepted practice when trying to understand a passage of Scripture, a "natural reading" of the text will be one that is in keeping with *the nature of the literature* you are dealing with and the context in which it occurs. In this case, the opening sentence of the introduction to Kidner's commentary reads, "The Old Testament repeatedly breaks out into poetry. Even its narratives are graced here and there with a couplet or a longer sequence of verse to make some memorable point (e.g., Genesis chapters 2 to 4 in any modern version), and its prophecies predominantly take this form. While the Psalms are the main body of poems in Scripture . . . they are themselves surrounded by poetry and rooted in a long and popular poetic tradition."[12]

Do have a look at what Derek Kidner writes. I think you will find that the language used in the book of the Psalms, being primarily poetic language, alerts one to the danger of reading into the text a meaning of specific words. This can happen either by projecting a meaning that our culture has held for some time and with which we have grown up or, as in this case, by equating a word with another word (in this instance, equating *soul* and *mind,* as in some philosophical writings), thus making them into the kind of language that you are familiar with in your scientific literature.

What I just said about being alert to the kind of language being used about human nature applies equally to the kinds of questions posed in Scripture. For example, two of the Psalms directly pose the question, What is a human being? (Psalms 8 and 144). Writing on Psalm 8, Derek Kidner says, "This Psalm is an unsurpassed example of *what a hymn should be*, celebrating as it does the glory and grace of God, rehearsing who He is and what He has done, and relating us and our world to him; all with a masterly economy of words, and in a spirit of mingled joy and awe."[13] This is quite different from what we should mean if we were asking in a scientific context, "What is a human being?" I commend what Derek Kidner has to say on this particularly because he underlines that Scripture is never asking an abstract question such as whether the soul is a separate thing.

A brief note, since I know you have the Inter-Varsity Press *New Bible Dictionary*[14]—may I suggest that you have a look at what it says there about the word *soul.* Among other things it quickly makes clear that if you look at the use of the word within the Psalms, which is what you mentioned, you will find that in different Psalms it is used in different ways. On one occasion it is the source of emotion; on another it is associated with the will and moral action; on another it is linked to physical appetite. And there are yet other passages where it designates an individual person. In other words, I don't think a comprehensive study of the way the word *soul* is used in the Psalms can constitute secure grounds for building a case for the soul as a separate thing.

Malcolm,

My other question was about how the soul is talked about in the New Testament, because any thoroughly biblical understanding we come to of the soul should take both the Old and New Testaments into account. What are your thoughts on the New Testament use of *soul?*

Ben,

Yes, I can do that by laying a bridge from your question about the Psalms to your further question about the New Testament. Let me just quote to you something written by another professor of Old Testament, this time Patrick Miller at Princeton Princeton Theological Seminary, in a chapter that he titled, "What Is a Human Being?" (with the subtitle "The Anthropology of Scripture"). He writes, "The human being under whom all things have been made subject (so Psalm 8) is the one who emptied himself, being born in human likeness (so Hebrews 2). The writer to the Hebrews hears in the Psalms the word that whatever we say about the human reality must take into account the face of Jesus Christ."[15]

Now to your question about the soul in the New Testament. There have been volumes on this in recent years, and I can point you to some of these if you wish. Most make the point that Christian teaching traditionally divided man into body, soul and spirit, what some people refer to as "the troublesome trichotomy theory." This certainly generates problems since close study shows that the differences, if any, between soul and spirit are not easy to define. Basically, the New Testament sees a person as consisting of a body (*soma*) and a soul (*psyche*). Although both taken together constitute the complete person as a unity, it is nevertheless possible to say that a man has a body (for example, 2 Corinthians 5:6: "We know that while we are at home in the body, we are away from the Lord") and that he is a soul or living being (for example, 1 Corinthians 15:45: "Thus it is written, 'The first man Adam became a living being'; the last Adam became a life-giving spirit").

The difficulty of distinguishing between the soul and the spirit arises in part from the different vocabularies of the New Testament writers. Paul, for instance, uses *pneuma* (for man's spirit) widely, but hardly ever uses *psyche*. John, on the other hand, never applies *pneuma* to man. All this adds up to the need to exercise caution when tempted to make dogmatic statements about what the soul is and is not.

So in answer to the question, Whatever happened to the soul? I think you'll discover that in contemporary translations of the Bible every attempt is made to steer us away from making the soul into a thing, a separate entity. Rather, we are encouraged to recognize that it refers to the whole living person. Thus, whereas in Luke 12:19 we used to read in the King James Version, "And I will say to my soul, Soul, . . .," we now read in, for example, the New English Bible, "I will say to myself, 'Man, . . .,'" or in the New International Version, "And I'll say to myself; 'You . . .'" In other words, it is the whole person, already enjoying a new life in Christ, who looks forward with confidence because, since Christ is risen, we also shall be raised with him. Not just our soul will be raised, but we shall be raised.

Malcolm,

You have certainly given me some things to think about. I'll have another look at Derek Kidner's commentary on the Psalms and also on the *New Bible Dictionary.*

I think I mostly understand by now your thoughts regarding mind and brain and what this means for our understanding of the relation of body and soul. But are there other views that hold a similar view of Scripture but that see the body-soul relationship differently? I would like to know how your view compares with these others. I want to be able to think through whether the views that are held by others on the mind-brain link have different implications for how we think about the body and the soul. Can you recommend anything to read on this?

Ben,

InterVarsity Press has come up with just what you need. They recently published *In Search of the Soul: Four Views of the Mind-Body Problem,* which offers you four different ways to think about the mind and brain in understanding the human person. The authors share a common commitment to giving primacy to Scripture, and they offer alternative views of how to see the scriptural stories about human nature in light of the relevant scientific accounts of human nature.[16]

Personally, I find the most convincing approach in this volume, in the sense of doing most justice both to the science and to Scripture, to be the one written by Nancey Murphy. She labels her view "Nonreductive Physicalism." If we must have labels put on us, I prefer to call my view dual-aspect monism, as I've mentioned before. By this I mean that there is only one reality to be understood and explained—this is what I would call the "mind-brain unity," hence the word *monism*. By saying "dual-aspect," I am affirming that in order to do full justice to the nature of this reality we need to give at least two accounts of it: an account in terms of its physical makeup and an account in terms of our mental or cognitive abilities. You cannot reduce the one to the other. This may seem like a linguistic quibble, but my concern is that the term *physicalism,* as Nancey Murphy uses it, could be taken by some as giving precedence to the physical aspect of our makeup over the mental. I think that would be to ignore that, as I said earlier, we can only know and talk about the mind-body problem by using language and the mental categories it employs. So in this sense at least, not selecting out either the mental or the physical would avoid giving precedence to either. If pressed, I would say that referring only to the physical, as in Nonreductive Physicalism, runs the risk of seeming to endorse a materialist view which, in turn, implies that the mind is "nothing but" the chattering of the cells of the brain.

Incidentally, Joel Green wrote an excellent opening chapter to this book, called "Body and Soul, Mind and Brain." Green, a New Testament biblical scholar, addresses how the soul is talked about in the New Testament and how that fits with what we have noticed in the Old Testament, which will likely interest you. Do let me know what you make of it all.

Malcolm,

We have covered so many different topics related to understanding the Bible, some of it rather technical. Can you offer me any guidelines for how properly to read and learn from Scripture?

Ben,

Today there is a very lively debate taking place between Christians equally committed to the importance of taking seriously all that Scripture says while doing full justice to the new insights we now have into how properly to interpret Scripture. For example, the Old Testament scholar Peter Enns, whom I have mentioned earlier, has emphasized that "it is a fundamental misunderstanding of Genesis to expect it to answer questions generated by a modern worldview, such as whether the days were literal or figurative, or whether the days of creation can be lined up with modern science, or whether the flood was local or universal. The question that Genesis is prepared to answer is whether Yahweh, the God of Israel, is worthy of worship."[17] Commenting on Enns's views, Mark Noll, in his very recent book *Jesus Christ and the Life of the Mind,* has helpfully stated:

> He follows in the long line of distinguished theologians and biblical scholars—including Augustine, Calvin, James Orr, Ned Stonehouse, and N. T. Wright among others—by concluding that biblical assertions may not mean the same as modern assumptions would dictate when it comes to matters like chronology; numbers; the relationship between recorded single speeches (e.g., the Sermon on the Mount) and what was actually said in one or more speeches, or what reflected a broad set of teachings communicated in many different ways; the mingling of what moderns would consider myth into what they would consider verifiable history; and the absence of clear markers in history-type writing to distinguish among what we in recent centuries have come to differentiate as theological, ethical, and historical writing.[18]

Malcolm,

The other day I was sharing with some friends who are doing courses in biblical studies what you had said about the soul and the changes in biblical interpretation over the years. One of them said that some people had attempted to use "depth psychology" as a new way of understanding and interpreting some parts of the Bible. I know that we don't really do any depth psychology in our courses apart from a brief mention of Freud, and even less about Jung, but is there anything here that I should be taking seriously in understanding what the Bible says?

Ben,

I wonder whether your friend's lecturers in the department of biblical studies had told him about a book that came out recently with the title *Psychology and the Bible: A New Way to Read the Scriptures.*[19] This book offers a range of psychological approaches to biblical interpretation. However, on closer examination they turn out to be almost exclusively based on depth psychologies. Not just Freud and Jung but some more recent ones like Erikson and Winnicott. The whole volume has a very strongly psychotherapeutic flavor. This brings to mind what I mentioned when we first started corresponding—that for many Christians the interest in psychology is focused primarily on things like pastoral psychology and counseling.

As Fraser Watts has wisely noted, "It is always right to be wary of any claim to have the psychological approach to a particular passage, and more appropriate to see it as one approach among a variety which may be possible."[20]

Malcolm,

That makes sense. But since the Bible talks so much about people and about God's dealings with people, I'm surprised that there haven't been more attempts to apply psychology to the interpretation of the Bible.

Ben,

Yes, it is rather surprising. But I think many biblical scholars and theologians have been reluctant to think psychologically about the Bible based on their objection to what they see as the essentially reductionistic nature of modern psychology.

But psychology need not of necessity be reductionistic. Very recently Joanna Collicutt has argued persuasively that there are areas of research in contemporary psychology that are indeed relevant to understanding the processes both of the production of biblical texts and of their interpretation and understanding. For example, she illustrates how the psychology of memory is extremely relevant to understanding the production of biblical texts, a point amplified in some detail by the biblical scholar Richard Bauckham in his book *Jesus and the Eyewitnesses.*[21] She also shows how social psychology has something to say about the production of sacred texts. And it is not just in the production of the texts but also in the way the texts are received where psychological research may have something to say. Here Collicutt refers to the theory of cognitive dissonance, and to evidence of the effects of systematic biases in information processing as examples. She also sees it possible to apply psychology in the exegesis of texts. I believe her argument is convincing and well worth taking seriously if you are interested in following this through.

Joanna Collicutt summarizes her approach admirably. She writes, "It has been argued that psychology is fundamentally about people and how they actually behave—how they think and remember, make and conserve meaning, attempt to communicate, process and express emotion, and exist in relation to others. Any approach to the Bible that does not pay due attention to the human factors, doing them the respect of applying rigorous methods to this study, is likely to be impoverished."[22] It will be most interesting to see how biblical scholars respond to Collicutt's thought-provoking paper.

Very recently a good friend who has spent many years working for Scripture Union—specifically helping Christians in nonwesternized countries, coming from different cultural backgrounds and, hence, with different presuppositions, produce Bible-reading study aids—drew my attention to a succinct and, I think, very helpful set of guidelines produced by an international group of Bible scholars. Scripture Union's Statement of Hermeneutical Principles states that Scripture should be interpreted prayerfully, corporately, as a whole, contextually (as it was written, how it is encountered and how it is lived out), Christologically and relationally. I encourage you to read through the statement in its entirety (see appendix).

As a footnote to this, since I believe you and your friends share a high regard for the writings of Jonathan Edwards, arguably the greatest North American theologian, may I draw your attention to something Edwards wrote centuries ago that directly addresses the issue of how to interpret Scripture. In a recent biography of Edwards, George Marsden wrote, "Edwards regarded Scripture alone as truly authoritative, so earlier interpreters could be revised. The project of understanding Scripture's true meaning was an ongoing progressive enterprise to which Edwards hoped to contribute."[23]

I think Edwards's highlighting of the ongoing nature of the enterprise is very important. It is Scripture that is authoritative, not the interpretation given by a particular group of Christians at a particular time. Though I understand and value the force of Edwards's views, I think I would like to clarify them and say further, as Tom Wright does, that it is God who is authoritative and who speaks through Scripture.[24] The title of Wright's book *Scripture and the Authority of God* squarely places our final authority on God, preeminently revealed in Jesus Christ.

8

Don't Parapsychology and Near-Death Experiences Prove the Existence of the Soul?

Malcolm,

I was chatting with some of my Christian friends the other day and telling them what you had told me about changing views of the soul, particularly among biblical scholars. Several said they thought the evidence from parapsychology and psychical research still "proved" that the soul was a separate nonphysical part of our nature. They were firm in their beliefs of a nonmaterial world of the spirit, as well as the existence of the soul, which could be set free from the physical body. They challenged the views you shared with me about the relation between mind and brain, arguing that the evidence from psychical research and parapsychology proved the dualist view of human nature with two separable parts, the body and the soul. They were all taught this view in their home churches and believe it to be biblical.

I know these are big questions, but I'm sure they'll come up again in conversation with my friends. Can you help me prepare by giving me your views on parapsychology and psychical research? Why doesn't it challenge your view of mind and brain being two aspects of a single unity?

Ben,

All very fair questions, especially in light of what I said earlier about the relation of mind and brain. I think it's highly unlikely you will get any lectures on parapsychology. That is not because no one takes the phenomena associated with parapsychology seriously—in fact, some psychology departments have set up research groups in parapsychology in recent years.

Rather, it is because there is so little time to fit everything in and, together with the bad name that parapsychology has gained for itself by the activities of charlatans and fraudsters, it is a good topic to leave out.

To clarify some terms, psychical research focuses, among other things, on connecting with the dead; parapsychology deals with whether there are people who can read other people's minds, who can see through brick walls with their minds or can foretell the future. A survey some years ago among the members of the United States National Academy of Sciences showed that 96 percent were skeptical that such phenomena exist. If extrasensory perception, or ESP, is real, it would mean that we have to overturn some of our widely accepted scientific understandings that our minds and physical brains are two aspects of a unified whole. I hasten to add that the history of science shows that, at times, new evidence does and can overturn scientific preconceptions, so we must keep an open, yet critical and well-informed mind on these issues.

Here is a brief account of my current views. Claims made about paranormal phenomena include *telepathy* (mind-to-mind communication where one person sends thoughts to another), *clairvoyance* (perception of remote events that are actually happening, such as that a friend has just had an accident) and *precognition* (perception of future events before they happen).

Regarding the last—seeing into the future—I think all the evidence currently available is clearly against this. If someone could demonstrate reliable precognition, stock exchange fund managers would be wanting to employ them, and they would be in great demand. Moreover, if there are such psychics, they let us down very badly on events such as 9/11. Likewise, no psychic came forward to collect a $50 million reward offered to locate Osama bin Laden after 9/11. Every attempt so far to test the prophetic powers of dreams have failed to produce any evidence in their support.

In some respects telepathy or ESP is a bit like phrenology, which I've mentioned before. When ESP is put to the experimental tests, it fails. Most scientists agree that with respect to parapsychology, generally what is needed is a reproducible phenomenon and a theory to explain it. As long ago as 1998 parapsychologist Rhea White concluded that "the image of parapsychology that comes to my mind, based on nearly 44 years in the field, is that of a small aeroplane that has been perpetually taxiing down the runway of the Empirical Science Airport since 1882, . . . its movement punctuated occasionally by lifting a few feet off the ground only to bump back down on the tarmac once again. It has never taken off for any sustained flight."[1]

With the advent of brain scanning machines, a new opportunity arose to test some of the claims of ESP. Harvard psychologists Samuel Mouton and Stephen Kosslynn did just this. They asked a "sender" to try and send one of two pictures telepathically to a "receiver" lying in an fMRI machine. The people involved were mostly couples or friends or twins who knew one another well. The results were just the same as in the past: the "receivers" guessed the pictures' content correctly at the level of chance, 50 percent. The researchers' conclusion was, "These findings are the strongest evidence yet obtained against the existence of paranormal mental phenomena."[2]

Earlier attempts to try to find evidence to support parapsychological phenomena had also failed. The high-profile American magician James Randi had offered $1 million "to anyone who proves a genuine psychic power under proper observing conditions." Similar large sums of money have been offered in other countries by other groups, but so far none of these large sums have been claimed. So it is not for want of trying. Randi's offer has been publicized for twelve years, and dozens of people have been tested under the scrutiny of an independent panel of judges, but so far nothing has emerged.

If you want to follow up some of the detailed evidence on this, I suggest a good place to start is in the psychology textbook you told me you were using by David Myers, where he has reviewed some of this evidence very succinctly.[3]

Malcolm,

I want to ask about your views on a related topic—one that seems to conflict with your view that mind and brain or soul and body cannot be separated. My Christian friends have been talking further about their beliefs regarding the soul, and they claim that they can use the evidence from so-called near-death experiences to "prove" that there is a separate realm of existence beyond this present one. Reports of near-death experiences "prove" that people's souls have left this present realm, briefly entered another realm and then returned. What do you think about using near-death experiences in that way?

Ben,

Reports of "near-death experiences" are varied. However, a typical account includes a number of essential ingredients. Here is one composite portrait of a typical near-death experience, courtesy of David Myers.

"A man hears himself pronounced dead by his doctor. . . . He feels himself moving very rapidly through a long dark tunnel—he finds himself outside of his own physical body—he sees his own body from a distance. Other things begin to happen—people come to help him—he glimpses the spirits of relatives and friends long since dead . . . a loving warm spirit of a kind he has never met before appears before him . . . he is overwhelmed by feelings of joy, love and peace. Despite all this however he is somehow reunited with his physical body and he lives."[4]

These are typical ingredients in the descriptions of near-death experiences given by those who've come close to death from cardiac arrest or other traumas. Depending on the study you look at, between 12 and 40 percent of people who come close to death from cardiac arrest and other traumas have reported a near-death experience.

What causes these kinds of experiences? The evidence currently available shows a variety of predisposing factors. At times people with temporal lobe epilepsy have reported profound mystical experiences with similarities to those of near-death experiences. Oxygen deprivation can also produce hallucinations with tunnel vision. One researcher has reported that since oxygen deprivation turns off the brain's inhibitory cells, neural activity increases in the visual cortex and in the oxygen-starved brain, resulting in a growing patch of light that looks much like what you would see as you move through a tunnel. One researcher concluded that the near-death experience is best understood as "hallucinatory reactivity of the brain."[5] Others who have investigated these experiences challenge this simple explanation, saying that people who have experienced both hallucinations and the near-death phenomena deny their similarity.

There are some parallels between these descriptions and the descriptions given by people who take hallucinogenic drugs. These drug users often also replayed old memories and saw visions of tunnels with bright lights. In other studies people experiencing near-death experiences describe visions of another world, although the content of the vision depends on the particular culture in which it occurs. So the debate will continue.

Malcolm,

Since near-death experiences are sometimes associated with brain malfunctions, it makes sense that they may not be as mysterious—opening doors into a nonmaterial world—as some people believe. But is it as simple as that? The apostle Paul once talked about having some kind of out-of-body experience. And aren't we told in the Old Testament about Samuel being called back from another world? What do you make of those episodes?

Ben,

Let's talk about Paul's experiences as recorded in his letter to the Corinthians. Here's what Paul wrote:

> It is necessary to boast; nothing is to be gained by it, but I will go on to visions and revelations of the Lord. I know a person in Christ who fourteen years ago was caught up to the third heaven—whether in the body or out of the body I do not know; God knows. And I know that such a person—whether in the body or out of the body I do not know; God knows—was caught up into Paradise and heard things that are not to be told, that no mortal is permitted to repeat. (2 Corinthians 12:1-4 NRSV)

In trying to understand this I would refer you to a leading New Testament scholar, Joel Green. He comments, "First, it is unlikely that Paul recounts in 2 Corinthians 12:1-4 an out-of-body experience since otherwise he might have reported with certainty that this 'vision and revelation' was indeed 'out of the body.' These studies lead to a second, ironic conclusion: out-of-body experiences are generated in our bodies, by our brains. Far from proving that there is an ethereal self that can separate itself from our material bodies, out-of-body experiences demonstrate rather the wonderful complexity of our brains as they situate us in time and space in ways that we mostly take for granted."[6]

I would add further that how you interpret experiences that occur as a result of the functioning of particular parts of the brain depends very much on the tradition within which you live, and in the beliefs you already hold. This was shown recently by Andrew Newberg and his colleagues, who have used single photon emission computed tomography, or SPECT brain imaging, to study the brains of people engaged in various forms of religious activities.[7] They found that accomplished Tibetan Buddhist meditators experienced a seemingly timeless and spaceless loss of differentiated sense of self. Among Christians such experiences are traditionally seen as a sense of mystical union with God, whereas among the Buddhists they would be experienced nonpersonally as Nirvana. How you interpret the experiences thus depends upon your presuppositions, not only on the specific activity of particular areas of your brain.

Malcolm,

But is there any recent evidence that provides any clues about the cause of out-of-body experiences? And if there is, what does it imply about what Paul reported?

Ben,

Yes, there is some recent evidence. Out-of-body experiences are typically brief episodes in which a person's conscious self seems to leave his body and look back at the body as that which belongs to them or to someone else. The evidence now shows that such out-of-body experiences are surprisingly common. Even within some Christian groups, such experiences are often looked upon as extremely valuable and are sought after. You may be surprised to know that one religious group in the U.S., in Oregon, has members who blend both the Christian and Brazilian indigenous religious beliefs and recently won the right to import and brew a hallucinogenic tea for its religious services. The tea is brewed with a particular plant, the ayahuasca plant, which contains trace amounts of the chemical dimethyltriptamine (or DMT), known to cause psychedelic phenomena including visual and audio sensations characteristic of an out-of-body experience.

Although many of us tend to think of out-of-body experiences as the product of a brain disorder like epilepsy or schizophrenia or the result of a hallucinogenic drug, most of the reports of such experiences have come from ordinary people in ordinary life circumstances.

Recent research by Henrick Ehrsson[8] has shown how out-of-body experiences can be created in healthy people without the use of drugs or electrical stimulation of the brain. He noted that one person in ten is thought to have undergone an out-of-body experience at some point in their life. Usually such events, where someone observes himself or herself from outside the physical body, are associated with traumatic experiences or situations where brain function is compromised, such as epilepsy or stroke. Ehrsson, working at the Wellcome Trust Centre for neuroimaging in London, used a video system to recreate out-of-body experiences in the laboratory. Experimental subjects watched head-mounted screens that showed them a live film of the back of the body, from the perspective of someone sitting behind them. The researchers then used two plastic rods, one to touch the subject's real chest and one to touch the "illusory chest" (just out of the camera's view). This triggered an out-of-body experience: subjects reported experiencing sitting behind their own body. When the illusory body was placed under threat, the participants physiological responses (skin perspiration) showed that they perceived this threat as real. The author of this report hopes that this kind of experiment will help to uncover the mechanisms behind why we associate our sense of self so closely with our physical bodies.

We are also beginning to gain a better understanding of which parts of the brain are primarily involved when these experiences occur—it is at the temporal parietal junction. Olaf Blanke, the Swiss neuroscientist I mentioned earlier, reported that when he had electrically stimulated a particular part of the brain, a patient who had no prior history of out-of-body experiences experienced one. The experiment was conducted with the patient fully awake and aware of her surroundings. She told the researchers she could now see the world, including herself lying on the bed, from an elevated perspective.[9]

And so I could go on, but the point I just want to make is that we are now beginning to understand a little more clearly the neural basis of these unusual experiences. So reported out-of-body experiences do not offer much support for the existence of a nonmaterial soul.

Malcolm,

Fascinating. And what about the Old Testament story of Samuel being called back again to this world?

Ben,

A word of caution. I think we sometimes expect short answers to seemingly simple questions about how to interpret Scripture, not realizing that there may be a long history of different interpretations down the centuries.

Samuel, so the account goes, is called up again from wherever he was by the witch or necromancer at Endor. Those who see this episode as proving that we have an immaterial immortal soul say that if Samuel's soul did in fact appear at Endor, then the so-called monist anthropology I have argued for, as consistent with both Scripture and science, is untenable and unscriptural. A challenge to take seriously.

I shall appeal to well-qualified biblical scholars in giving my answer. Let me share with you something I learned from a professor of Hebrew and Old Testament, Bill Arnold of Asbury Theological Seminary, talking about this passage.

Arnold explained that one group of early writers assumed that the figure at Endor was "not Samuel at all but only a delusional and deceptive apparition, having its origin in demonic forces and offering a forged prophecy."[10] Tertullian, for example, argued that the appearance was demonic, and he appealed to the apostle Paul's words in 2 Corinthians in support of his viewpoint. Paul writes, "Even Satan disguises himself as an angel of light. So it is not strange if his ministers also disguise themselves as ministers of righteousness" (2 Corinthians 11:14-15 NRSV). Arnold noted that many other early commentators quote Paul's text in a similar way, including Saint Augustine. There are yet other commentators from the first centuries of church history who take this view while not appealing to Paul's comments. Some better-known ones in this category are Gregory of Nyssa and Jerome.

Most of this group also take the view that it's not possible for a holy prophet to be disturbed and raised from the dead by necromantic rituals. So these early Christian thinkers concluded that the demon or Satan himself deceived Saul and the woman by appearing as Samuel. Arnold tells us that most critical commentaries of that time declined even to speculate about such possibilities. Others, in extreme attempts to, as he puts it, "square the text with one's theology," resorted to such creative explanations as the use of hallucinogenic narcotics or a psychological ecstatic trance that occurs without the benefit of such mind-altering drugs. As you see, given a little ingenuity, it is not difficult to come up with an alternative story.

A second group of early writers on this passage in 1 Samuel assumed that the appearance of Samuel was real. They believed that Samuel himself appeared at Endor, resurrected by God or by the woman through efficacious but illicit necromantic practices. For example, Justin Martyr argued for the existence and survival of the human soul based on this text. Other authors who assumed Samuel actually appeared at Endor include the historian Josephus as well as Origen and Ambrose. Saint Augustine seemed to change his views at different stages of his life on whether he thought Samuel himself appeared or, as I mentioned earlier, that a delusive demon appeared instead, but his conviction in later life seemed to favor the latter.

In a sense these details are not so important. What is important is that experts at different times in the church's history dealing with the same texts may come to radically different interpretations. Nothing new there. It happened with enormous consequences at the time of the Reformation.

Arnold believes that the ancient and classical authorities who took Samuel's appearance at Endor as a resuscitated physical body were closer to the ancient Israelites' perceptions and that such interpretations therefore do not require the existence of a disembodied, intermediate state of the dead Samuel.

I'll give a quick summary of Professor Arnold's views. He reminds us that, in interpreting any text of Scripture, we do well to pay attention to the history of interpretation before we undertake a contemporary examination of the exegetical issues of the text. He does this and describes how believers in antiquity read the account of Samuel's appearance at Endor. Against that background he explores the implications of this text and other data from the Hebrew Scriptures generally for the current debate about human nature. In answer to the question he poses—whether the text portrays a disembodied human soul—he concludes that those who assumed that it was the resuscitated physical body, not a disembodied soul, are closer to the original intent of the passage. And he goes on, "In other words, if ancient Israelites were faced with the question before us, I believe that they would respond, 'of course there is no existence apart from the physical.' Therefore Samuel's appearance at Endor, once accepted as real and not delusional, must be accepted as in some sense physical."[11]

Moving on to ask what the reading of this text would look like in the light of today's new biblical hermeneutics, he concludes, "This text represents a vestige of the customs and religious practices of Canaanites and some Israelites, despite the disapproval of normative Old Testament religion." But at no point does Professor Arnold suggest a new exegesis provides a knockdown argument in favor of either dualism or monism. He notes, rather, "Like other data from the Hebrew Scriptures this passage must ultimately remain inconclusive in matters of Christian anthropology, although the concept of physical resuscitation is suggestive."[12]

So although a superficial reading of 1 Samuel 28 may lead some of today's Christians to interpretations that appear to refute monist anthropology, believers from earliest times have disagreed about this difficult text, and no consensus can possibly emerge from here as defending a traditionalist dualism. I believe we should give closer attention to the Bible's phenomenological language with reference to the nature of human beings. When the text makes reference to the process of human thought, there is a conspicuous absence of "brain" language, and perhaps it is instructive to point out that biblical Hebrew has no word for "brain."

I suspect that you will feel that I have gone on a bit about this. My reason for doing so is that I believe that the data from the Hebrew Scriptures ultimately remain inconclusive in matters of constructing a Christian anthropology, although my own view is that the main thrust is toward a holistic view of the human person where the concept of physical resuscitation is important. I hope it will alert you to the need to be vigilant when views that are claimed to be knockdown arguments taken from a particular reading of a specific Scripture passage are put forward to suggest either (1) a direct conflict between science and Scripture or (2) that science is disproved by Scripture or vice versa.

I can quite understand that for someone who is not a Christian and does not have "the sure hope" and promise that we have—that since Christ rose we also shall be raised with him—it would be comforting to believe that there is another world to which they go after death and where they will meet loved ones already dead. Perhaps if Freud were listening to our conversation, he would add that that is the sort of belief that he sees as typical "wishful thinking." Looking for "evidence," I can see how the study of near-death experiences will continue to be a source of fascination and, for some, comfort. So watch this space! In the meantime we shall continue to affirm, as in the Apostles' Creed, our belief in resurrection: that as our human essence—our identity and consciousness—is embodied now, so in the resurrection we shall still be embodied, which is variously referred to as our "glorified" bodies or our "spiritual" bodies. But embodied. Not disembodied something-or-others drifting around in limbo. Not dependent on the dualisms of parapsychology and near-death experiences.

9

What Makes Us Human?

The Development of Evolutionary Psychology

Malcolm,

Evolutionary psychology is a big topic in my courses this term. When I mentioned this to my Christian friends, I got some of the same worried looks I saw earlier when I told them I was doing a minor course in evolutionary biology. Obviously they're suspicious of any course with the word *evolution* in its title. So I may need some help this term in responding to their concern.

Ben,

I think I understand why some of your Christian friends raise an eyebrow when they hear you are taking courses in evolutionary psychology, given some of the tendentious media interpretations of scientific discoveries. You don't have to be a psychology student to be puzzled and challenged by some of the media reporting. Of course television programs and glossy magazines are crafted to gain maximum publicity, so some of them come into the "gee-whiz" category.

To claim that the research findings of evolutionary psychologists necessarily challenge, for example, widely shared religious beliefs about the uniqueness of human beings is understandably worrying, especially if you don't have the knowledge to properly evaluate them and to refute them when they are wrong. I have in mind exaggerated claims that humans are "nothing but" rather sophisticated and advanced chimpanzees. But your current course will give you up-to-date specialist knowledge so that you can help some of your friends who are unsettled by these media reports.

Malcolm,

Why is evolutionary psychology in the limelight today? I assume it has been around at least since Darwin's day, so why are science and the media focusing on it only in the last few years?

Ben,

A bit of background helps. Yes, evolutionary psychology does link up with Darwin's theory of natural selection—it is the study of the evolution of behavior and the mind using principles of natural selection.

In 1992, John Tooby and Leda Cosmides defined evolutionary psychology as "psychology informed by the fact that the inherited structure of the human mind is a product of evolutionary processes."[1] The presumption is that natural selection favored genes that engendered both behavioral tendencies and information-processing systems that solved survival problems faced by our ancestors, thus contributing to the spread of their genes. Thus, one main focus of research in evolutionary psychology remains the question of how humans came to be the special animal that we are.

Questions asked by evolutionary psychologists are not new. Wiser people than us have asked similar questions in earlier generations. This point was made in a recent review of *Good Natured,* one of the widely read books on evolutionary psychology, written by Frans de Waal, a leader in the field. The review began, "From the beginning philosophers have agonized over the question of what makes us human. Is there a difference in kind or merely a difference in degree between ourselves and other animals?" It went on, "Direct comparisons between people and animals are often seen as demeaning, even offensive."[2]

You may ask if the very attempt to pose such questions is out of bounds for Christians. I think not. We need to remember that human-animal comparisons are not new, even within theological circles. The outstanding mathematician, thinker and committed Christian Blaise Pascal wrote in 1659, "It is dangerous to show a man too clearly how much he resembles the beast, without at the same time showing him his greatness. It is also dangerous to allow him too clear a vision of his greatness without his baseness. It is even more dangerous to leave him in ignorance of both."[3] Evolutionary psychology can certainly help to reduce that ignorance.

Malcolm,

What are your thoughts about the scientific basis of evolutionary psychology? Since evolutionary psychology is a relatively recent major development in psychology, do you feel it has a secure enough scientific foundation for us as Christians to be reexamining some of our long-held beliefs in light of its claims?

Ben,

I believe that the scientific foundations of evolutionary psychology are becoming more secure all the time. But that does not mean that there will not be radical changes brought about by fresh evidence from experimental and empirical studies. There will be. That is how science progresses.

My impression is that evolutionary psychologists who are at the cutting edge in research are, for the most part, much more cautious about making excessive, unwarranted claims. In particular, they are cautious when speculating about the wider significance of any research they are reporting. It is the media who want a good story, who will pick up on bits of research and report it with eye-catching headlines.

I hope and imagine that some of your other lecturers will remind you that evolutionary psychology is only one part of contemporary psychology. This needs to be said because today some psychologists are so enthused by evolutionary psychology that they see it as mounting a take-over bid for the whole of psychology. For example, David Buss subtitled his book *Evolutionary Psychology,* published in 2000, *The New Science of the Mind.*[4] He then proceeded to reorganize the whole of psychology within an overall framework of evolutionary psychology. Others are more modest in their claims. For example, courses in the Open University in Britain are content simply to note that "Evolutionary psychology focuses on how human beings came to be the apparently special animal we are today."

More recently one of the leaders in the field in Britain, Robin Dunbar, professor of evolutionary anthropology at Oxford University, has argued that debates over the role of evolutionary psychology have been largely misplaced. He thinks that some of the ways in which evolutionary psychology has been presented has led to an "adverse reaction on the part of more conventional psychologists" and given rise to an unnecessary and "fractious debate." He thinks it's a dispute that has been "largely misplaced."[5] I agree with him.

Recently Dunbar wrote, "One reason for this misunderstanding has been a seemingly inevitable tendency for psychologists to interpret an evolutionary approach in terms of the nature/nurture debate." This then gets linked to highly charged topics such as genetic differences between races, genders or even social classes. He continues,

> A second source of confusion has been the fact that psychologists are used to explaining human behaviour in terms of motivations. So when evolutionary psychologists assert that someone behaves in a particular way "in order to maximise their fitness," this has often been interpreted as a statement about what actually motivates people. . . . In fact, this is to confuse apples with oranges. Evolutionary explanations are about the ultimate (i.e., evolutionary) goals that guide behaviour, not their immediate motivations. Such explanations lie at a higher explanatory level: evolutionary goal states require motivations to make them possible.[6]

Notice here that he talks about "explanations at different levels" and this is something that has to be kept in mind all the time when discussing human behavior.

You may remember that I mentioned levels of explanation when we were talking about links between brain processes and religious experience and behavior. Dunbar goes on, "The problem is that both these common responses conflate different levels . . . of explanation. . . . Certainly, there must be genes involved, but these genes need not be genes that determine behaviour, or even the mind in fine detail."[7]

Malcolm,

Yes, I've heard quite a lot about Robin Dunbar. He seems to be very important in the field of evolutionary psychology. Are you familiar with "Dunbar's number"?

Ben,

Yes, I am familiar with the term. In fact, Dunbar provides a definition for "Dunbar's number" in the article I've been quoting for you. He describes it as "the apparently universal typical size of social circles at around 150 individuals." Here's another quote from the article, which illustrates, once again, the need to recognize how we study phenomena at different levels.

> The point of this example [Dunbar's number] is that it shows how understanding a fairly simple phenomenon—how many friends we have—can, within an evolutionary framework, allow us to integrate a wide range of different subdisciplines. Here, we fitted together a jigsaw of components based on differences in social behaviour, their cognitive, neurological and developmental underpinnings, and their social consequences both for the individual and for the emergent structural aspects of society as well as something to do with the functions of group life. We have slipped effortlessly from neuropsychology to sociology, and back, and called in on ecology on the way.[8]

I think this example serves to underline the way in which many different disciplines contribute to the understanding of behavior, and that evolutionary psychology is just one of the specialist areas to make a contribution. So we need to keep in mind the different levels of explanation at which any particular piece of behavior can be analyzed and studied. That is a pervasive theme today in all of psychology. When we forget that there are these different levels of explanation and begin to muddle them up, then we create all sorts of unnecessary problems.

Malcolm,

I've been thinking more about our discussion of evolutionary psychology and what makes us human. One of the things that comes up repeatedly in our lectures is the overlap between the problem-solving behavior of chimpanzees and very young children. But doesn't that contradict what it seems to me the Bible teaches—namely, that we are unique in all of creation? How do we bear in mind the similarities between animals and humans, while at the same time doing justice to the differences?

Ben,

You ask about our uniqueness. Is it real or illusory? We need to remember that animals of each phylum are unique. Each has properties and abilities none other does (e.g., birds fly; we cannot). There are other claims to uniqueness that lie outside the domain of science—for example, the faith claim that humans alone, in all creation, are offered God's gracious invitation to have a personal relationship with him. Evolutionary psychology, as part of science, has no interest in such a question and no views on it. That is not to say that individual psychologists will not have personal beliefs about such wider issues. They will and they do.

There are some topics widely discussed today by evolutionary psychologists that lend themselves readily to misunderstanding because the language they use is not as clearly technical as, for example, the language you have come across in your neuroscience course. I have in mind two particular areas of contemporary evolutionary psychology: mind reading and altruistic behavior. Both are actively researched by scientists and both get a lot of media interest. They are not unrelated, and altruistic behavior potentially overlaps with topics before seen as the domain of philosophers and theologians. Once that happens you have the ingredients for confusion, unless great discipline is exercised and care taken to make clear whether you are making a theological affirmation or reporting a scientific finding. Altruistic love, for example, is a pervasive theme in Scripture. But what Scripture is saying is not to be regarded as the kind of statement that would describe altruistic behavior in animals in a journal of social and behavioral neuroscience.

Research on mind reading, another name for "theory of mind," goes back to the ideas of Premack and Woodruff in 1978. They described animals who had the ability to understand the mind of another animal as possessing a "theory of mind."[9] As Whiten has written, "Theory of mind refers to the everyday psychology that we use to understand and explain our own and others' actions, by reference to mental states such as 'knowing' and 'believing.'"[10] Whiten further writes that "'Mindreading' provides a useful verb—to mindread—and tends to be preferred by those who dislike talk of 'theory' when we are just talking about people's everyday ideas about 'mind,' rather than the science of psychology."[11]

The topic of mind reading well illustrates how important it is to remember that when a field is advancing very rapidly, the prudent scientist, however enthusiastic about his science, nevertheless knows from his knowledge of the history of science that, at times, supposedly well-established and widely held views can change rapidly in light of new evidence. This was illustrated recently by advances in research on theory of mind. It used to be argued that it is only humans who have a theory of mind. Up until 2000, Michael Tomasello, a lead researcher, believed that the observational data reported by my friends and colleagues here at St Andrews, Richard Byrne and Andrew Whiten, claiming to show forms of rudimentary mind reading in chimpanzees, was not convincing evidence that nonhuman primates have a theory of mind. Today, Tomasello, on the basis of his own laboratory studies, is convinced that his earlier views were wrong and in need of revision. In 2003 Tomasello wrote:

> In our 1997 book *Primate Cognition* we reviewed all the available evidence and concluded that nonhuman primates understand much about behavior of conspecifics but nothing about their psychological states, [but] . . . in the last five years new data have emerged that require modification of this hypothesis. The form that a new hypothesis should take is not entirely clear, but we are now convinced that at least some nonhuman primates—the research is mainly on chimpanzees—do understand at least some psychological states in others. . . . For the moment we feel safe in asserting that chimpanzees can understand some psychological states in others, the question is only which ones and to what extent.[12]

More recently, in October 2010, Tomasello published another paper in which he reported giving a comprehensive battery of cognitive tests to three groups: a large number of chimpanzees, a group of orangutans and a large group of two-and-a-half-year-old children. The test battery apparently consisted of a whole lot of different nonverbal tasks designed to assess cognitive skills, involving physical and social problems. Tomasello and his colleagues found that, as reported in the past, the children and the apes show similar skills when dealing with the physical world, but already by age two and a half the children had more sophisticated cognitive skills than either of the ape species studied when it came to dealing with the social world. "Distinct species-unique skills" of what the researchers called social cognition had emerged in the children by age two and a half.[13]

So there's an example where it is sensible to take note of the overlapping skills between animals and humans but equally important to take note of the clear differences that emerge. The paper by Tomasello very nicely makes the point that the leaders in evolutionary psychology are extremely sensitive to the need to be aware of the uniqueness of humans. I rather suspect that, in the next decade or two, the emphasis in some areas of research in evolutionary psychology will change from documenting in ever greater detail the overlaps and similarities between the cognitive achievements and behaviors of animals and humans, to identifying instead the unique features of human cognition and behavior. One reason I suspect that the research may move in this direction is that given the significant similarities between the brains of humans and nonhuman primates, there has been a tendency in the past to ignore the extremely puzzling question of how it is that with such similar brains to their nonhuman primate ancestors, humans nevertheless are totally different from any of them. Whoever went to Africa to study a group of nonhuman primates and found they had hospitals, libraries, technology parks, art galleries, churches, symphony orchestras and so on and so on? You see my point. It is so easy to gloss over these enormous and fundamental differences, but the question is why, with such similar brains, are we so totally different?

Malcolm,

That's really interesting. I'd like to hear more about how the mind-reading behavior you mentioned has been shown to be present in both humans and chimpanzees. Can you think of an example from recent research that illustrates this?

Ben,

Yes, here is an example from the work of Richard Byrne, one of my colleagues at St Andrews. Some researchers, making links with neuroscience, have argued that clever-looking behavior in some nonhuman primates, which looks like mind reading in humans, results from a rapid increase in neocortical volume. They show that there is a direct relationship between neocortical volume and amount of (clever-looking) behaviors. That applies to deception, to innovation and to tool use. Richard Byrne wrote,

> Quite what benefits a large neo-cortex brings—the underlying cognitive basis of monkey and ape social sophistication—is not straightforward to answer. It is tempting, but may be utterly wrong, to assume that an animal that works over many months to build-up a friendly relationship has some idea of the effect its behavior is having on the mind of the other. . . . We assume the agent realizes that by producing a false belief in his victim may

> risk losing a friend or gaining an enemy. The alternative is a more prosaic mixture of genetic predisposition and rapid learning—and often this is more likely. . . . Researchers have to be very cautious, then, in attributing to nonhuman primates the ability to understand social behavior or how things work in the mechanistic way of adult humans. . . . Rapid learning in circumstances, a good memory for individuals and their different characteristics, and some simple genetic tendencies are capable of explaining much that has impressed observers as intelligent in simian primates.[14]

Most recently the results of research by evolutionary psychologists have been discussed in another context where serious ethical and medical issues arise. In 2011 the Academy of Medical Sciences in Britain published the results of studies of current and possible future use of animals containing human material.[15] Their report considers research involving the introduction of human DNA sequence into animals, on the mixing of human and animal cells or tissues, to create entities referred to as "animals containing human material." In the part of their report titled "Future Science and Implications," they try to look ahead, noting that already animal models of human diseases involving the brain have been developed, such as those where transgenic mice are used to study dementias. Another example is where rats are engrafted with human neural stem cells to study the potential of these cells for repairing damage caused by strokes. The report highlights how the extension of such research methods into nonhuman primates sharpens up the ethical issues. They provide a summary of "Aspects of brain function that may distinguish humans and the Great Apes from other species."[16] Note how they grouped together humans and the Great Apes, once more underlying our major question, "What makes us different?"

So you see there are serious scientific issues to be addressed here, and it may be tempting, in a search for human uniqueness, to seize upon something that sounds very human, such as mind reading, as a way of uniquely separating off humans from nonhumans. Equally tempting, when we find close similarities between the behavior of humans and some nonhuman primates, is to say that humans are therefore "nothing but" unusually complex primates and to ignore the distinctiveness of the ethical, moral and religious aspects of human cognition and behavior and the "quantum leap" in problem solving between an Einstein and a very clever ape. It seems that when discussing issues at the interface of science and faith there is this ever-present temptation to slip into unthinking reductionism. All this despite the clear statements of leading scientists warning against it. They realize that it can foreclose further work on key issues such as the relation between mental life and its physical substrates.

Malcolm,

Is it possible that you're overstating the case against reductionism? Surely if we can give an explanation of a behavior at a more basic level—say, in terms of the activity of neurons in the brain or biochemistry of the brain—that is more satisfying than an explanation that has been given in terms of things like motivation?

Ben,

Good question. Your way of expressing it puts you in elevated company. Some very distinguished scientists have believed that scientific descriptions can reduce human life, including religion, to nothing more than biological or physical processes. You will recall that in our discussion on how to relate "mind talk" to "brain talk," we noted that Francis Crick, the Nobel Laureate and arguably one of the greatest biologists of the last century, revealed in his book *The Astonishing Hypothesis* a firm commitment to such unrelenting reductionism, what some have called "nothing buttery," in his writing. He wrote, "You are no more than the behavior of a vast assembly of nerve cells and their associated molecules. . . . You're nothing but a pack of neurons."[17] We noted that the problem is that the logical conclusion to Crick's own argument would have to be that his own written words about his Astonishing Hypothesis were "nothing but" ink strokes on the page, carrying no message. Even he drew back at the end of the book, saying, "The words 'nothing but' in our hypothesis can be misleading if understood in too naive a way."[18]

I must stop now, but if you want me to say a bit about altruism, which is frequently in the news today regarding close similarities between humans and animals, I can do so another day. Since it is something that, in some of its forms, is talked about in Scripture, I can see why it is perhaps a more emotionally loaded topic than mind reading.

10

Are Humans Different?

What About Morality in Animals?

Malcolm,

My evolutionary psychology course continues to raise new questions for me. Last week we had three lectures on the evidence for the possibility of cultures in animals. But I thought only humans create culture. Do you know of recent research on this issue of animal cultures?

Ben,

Your lecturers are certainly up to date. There is a developing literature on whether animals have what are variously called *traditions* and *cultures*.

In 2005 my colleague Andrew Whiten, with Victoria Horner and Frans de Waal, published a paper in the journal *Nature* with the title "Conformity to Cultural Norms of Tool Use in Chimpanzees."[1] They reported studying a subset of chimpanzees that discovered a method of tool use that matched a predominant approach of their companions and showed a conformity bias that is regarded as a hallmark of human culture.

More recently, in 2010, another researcher, this time from McMaster University in Canada, published a paper in the journal *Dispatches* titled "Animal Traditions: Experimental Evidence of Learning by Imitation in an Unlikely Animal."[2] The researchers studied mongooses, animals not normally regarded as close to us from an evolutionary point of view. They opened their report with the sentence, "The possibility that nonhuman animals living in natural environments have 'culture' has been of great recent interest." Their research demonstrated that social learning can maintain behavioral traditions in a single population.

Malcolm,

Since humans in different cultures often have different moral codes, does this recent research imply that animals who have traditions also make moral judgments? And do animals have "moral codes"? If they do, does that mean that another difference between us and animals has gone?

Ben,

A timely question. Morality was discussed recently in a paper by Francisco Ayala, one of America's leading evolutionary biologists.[3] He accepts that humans are animals that have evolved from ancestors that were not human. Nonetheless, we have developed capacities (including mental capacities) that make us a unique kind of animal—a unique kind of ape, with its own distinctive features. One of these features, he believes, is the moral sense. That understanding morality is an important contemporary issue finds support from Harvard psychologist Steven Pinker, who wrote, "Morality is not just any old topic in psychology but close to our conception of the meaning of life. Moral goodness is what gives each of us the sense that we are worthy human beings."[4]

Ayala argues that the relative sizes and complexities of chimpanzee and ape brains when compared with human adult brains are a key factor in understanding the most fundamental changes of all, the intellectual faculties that humans show. These, he says, have allowed us to categorize, to think abstractly, to form images of realities that are not presently in front of us, and to reason.

He also suggests some other distinctive functional features in humans, though I'm not sure the evidence for these is so strong. He includes self-awareness and death awareness, but I wonder how he knows these things. I think he's on safer ground when he talks about symbolic language, but again on rather weaker ground when he talks about tool making. Where he is on very strong ground, however, is the enormous—and I really mean enormous—differences between human societies and any animal societies in terms of the development of science, literature, art, ethics and religion.

Malcolm,

What does Ayala mean by "moral sense"? That must be important.

Ben,

Ayala thinks that talk about moral sense is a way of referring to how someone takes into account, in a sympathetic way, the impact one's actions will have on others. This, I'm sure you'll quickly notice, links up with discussions of altruism, which in turn link up with empathy, sympathy and consolation. Ayala says, "Altruism may be defined . . . as unselfish regard for or devotion to the welfare of others."[5]

Ayala goes a step further. He sees morality and ethics as synonymous. Against this background he asks questions such as, Did modern humans have an ethical sense from the beginning? Did Neanderthals hold moral values? What about Homo erectus and Homo habilis? How did the moral sense evolve? Was it directly promoted by natural selection? These are difficult questions.

Ayala believes that the clue to understanding how humans differ from nonhuman primates is to be found in the difference between what he and fellow evolutionary biologists call *adaptations* and *exaptations*. He says,

> Evolutionary biologists define exaptations as features of organisms that evolved because they served some function but are later co-opted to serve an additional or different function, which was not originally the target of natural selection. The new function may replace the older function or coexist together with it. Feathers seem to have evolved first for conserving temperature, but were later co-opted in birds for flying. . . . The issue at hand is whether moral behavior was directly promoted by natural selection or rather it is simply a consequence of our *exalted intelligence*, which was the target of natural selection (because it made possible the construction of better tools). Art, literature, religion, and many human cultural activities might also be seen as *exaptations* that came about as consequences of *the evolution of high intelligence*.[6]

So for Ayala, the human moral sense is an exaptation, not an adaptation, and the target of natural selection was the development of advanced intellectual capacities. Later he suggests that the moral sense that had evolved as an exaptation associated with high intelligence could eventually become an adaptation, by favoring beneficial behaviors. He applies a similar argument to the development of ethics.

> The capacity for ethics is an outcome of gradual evolution, but it is an attribute that only exists when the underlying attributes (i.e., the intellectual capacities) reach an advanced degree. The necessary conditions for ethical behavior only come about after the crossing of an evolutionary threshold. The approach is gradual, but the conditions only appear when the degree of intelligence is reached such that the formation of abstract concepts and the anticipation of the future are possible, even though we may not be able to determine when the threshold was crossed.[7]

For Francisco Ayala, then, moral codes come about as a result of cultural evolution, which he sees as a distinctive mode of evolution that has surpassed the biological mode because it is a more effective form of adaptation; it is faster than biological evolution and can be directed. Ayala's views converge with those of neuroscientists. In 2011 a leading philosopher of neuroscience, Patricia Churchland, published a book titled *Braintrust: What Neuroscience Tells Us About Morality*.[8] When Adina Roskies reviewed Churchland's book in *Nature*, she noted how Churchland "argues that human moral behaviour emerges from the mechanisms that evolved to promote social interactions" and that Churchland further argues that "it is misleading to conceive of morality as innate, genetically specified or associated with one module in the brain."[9]

My own brief footnote on these views of Ayala and Churchland would be to note first the importance of the concept of emergence and second yet another warning about not looking for a "God module" in the brain. We shall, I suspect, return to emergence later in our conversations.

Malcolm,

You seem to place a lot of weight on Ayala's analysis of how moral behavior evolved. Are there other views that are important to know about?

Ben,

Yes, there are indeed. Around the time that Francisco Ayala's paper appeared, a symposium was published under the title *Does Moral Action Depend on Reasoning?*[10] It contained answers to this question by philosophers, lawyers, theologians and neuroscientists. Certain themes emerged from their answers that are helpful in assessing Ayala's arguments.

Malcolm,

I was discussing with some friends what you told me about Ayala's views. One said he heard that Ayala had won the Templeton prize for religion recently, and that he is a Christian. This friend, who isn't a Christian, said he'd like to hear the views of other people who are not Christian. So, for example, do other leading scientists also believe that we are free to choose and develop our own moral code? What do neuroscientists think about this? And philosophers, and psychologists?

Ben,

You asked for it, so here it is.

The neuroscientists in the Templeton Symposium agreed about the implications of their discipline. Michael Gazzaniga lists different views currently circulating in the intellectual marketplace of these issues. One view claims that there are "inherent moral modules . . . thought to be the product of evolution and to represent optimal responses, from the point of view of natural selection, to matters dealing with purity, cheating, killing, and the like." However, he acknowledges, "Other theorists argue that it is through experience and culture that we learn how to play by the rules of our social group. As we accumulate this conscious knowledge, the decision networks in our brains learn the various costs and benefits of different actions, and our moral behavior emerges through a traditional learning pattern. Adherents to this view see our social environment as the dominant factor in the development of our moral behavior."[11] This seems very close to the views put forward by Ayala. (Though I am worried by Gazzaniga's sloppy use of language. Our brains are physical machines. They don't learn about costs and benefits—we do.)

Gazzaniga concludes,

> These recent advances in understanding how the brain works in producing moral behavior do not challenge or make obsolete the value of holding people in a society accountable for their actions. Though it does suggest that the endless historical discussion of free will and the like has little or no meaning, it does not suggest in any way that we, as mental agents, are merely accessory to our brain activity. *Indeed, in beginning to understand how the mind emerges from the brain, we are also realizing how the mind constrains the brain.*[12]

Malcolm,

Thanks for the helpful outline of Churchland's and Gazzaniga's views. What do other neuroscientists think?

Ben,

Neurologist Antonio Damasio's answer to the question posed in the symposium is, "Yes and no." *Yes* because he believes that "actions we can truly call moral depend on the work of reason at some stage"; *no* because "the moment-to-moment execution of actions, moral or otherwise, is not necessarily under the control of reason, even if reason has a role in the deliberations behind the action and in strengthening the control system that executes it."[13]

Malcolm,

I'm curious whether the neuroscientists or psychologists at the symposium discussed psychopathology? One of our lecturers showed some pictures from brain-scanning studies comparing the brains of psychopaths with those of normal people and demonstrating clear differences between the brains of the two groups when they were confronted with making moral decisions. If the evidence is showing that the brains of psychopaths are in some cases different from the brains of the rest of the population, in what sense can we hold them responsible for their behavior and any moral decisions they make that seem right to them but unacceptable to us? This seems to be a key problem facing people who want to say that we are entirely free to behave just as we wish and that we should be held fully responsible for every aspect of our behavior.

Ben,

The symposium did have a contribution on psychopathology. Psychologist Jonah Lehrer pointed out that one of the outstanding features of psychopaths is their lack of concern about widely culturally shared moral judgments. Lehrer asked the question, What's gone wrong with the psychopaths? He notes that often they are highly intelligent people with excellent language skills, so "why are psychopaths so much more likely to use violence to achieve their goals? Why are they so overrepresented in our prisons? The answer points us to the anatomy of morality in the mind. That's because the intact intelligence of psychopaths conceals a devastating problem: the emotional parts of their brains are damaged, and this is what makes them dangerous."[14]

This is relevant, since according to Ayala's argument, it was the evolution and development of the brain that gave rise to the advanced intelligence of humans, but Lehrer makes the point that such advanced intelligence is no guarantee of moral behavior if the emotional parts of the brain are damaged. Lehrer writes, "When you peer inside the psychopathic brain, you can literally see this absence of emotion. After being exposed to fearful facial expressions, the emotional parts of the normal human brain show increased levels of activation. . . . The brains of psychopaths, however, respond to these fearful faces with utter disinterest. Their emotional areas are unperturbed, and their facial recognition system is even *less* interested in fearful faces than in perfectly blank stares. Their brains are bored by expressions of terror."[15]

Lehrer comments further, "Neuroscientists are beginning to identify the specific deficits that define the psychopathic brain," adding later, "in other words, *it is the absence of emotion*—and not a lack of rationality—that makes the most basic moral concepts incomprehensible to them."[16]

Malcolm,

Thank you. The contribution on psychopathology certainly fits with what we've been taught in our lectures.

What do you think about all this? In your opinion, does the evidence of some forms of morality among animals undermine human distinctiveness? And what is the contribution of science to studying human distinctiveness, as compared with the contribution from other disciplines, including the Bible?

Ben,

I think we can rest assured that scientific research into human distinctiveness will continue among scientists. As I illustrated earlier, properly used in things like biomedical research it has potentially great benefits for human well-being. Research into what exactly are the distinctive marks of humans will produce many surprises along the way. However, the appearance of what we might call a fuzzy boundary between humans and animals is not something that should bother Christians and those holding a religious outlook on life. For many of those who do not believe in God, there is a tacit acceptance that humans are clearly unique in terms of their explosive development of learning, philosophy, literature, music, art, science, religion and so on. Perhaps what some recent science developments have done is warn us off trying to base our claims of human uniqueness on such things as human capacity for thinking or reasoning. Both depend on how you define them, and can be seen at least in rudimentary form in animals. I don't see any great issues at stake here for Christians. For us as Christians, the important aspects of human uniqueness are based on theological presuppositions, not on neurobiological observations.

We may indeed, and quite rightly, be as concerned as good scientists are about some of the popular exaggerations that appear in the media when reporting developments in the study of animal behavior. As Christians I think we should be enthusiastically open-minded about developments in evolutionary psychology—not gullible, but discerning—and in them glimpsing fresh pointers to the greatness of the Creator as seen in the wonders of his creation.

When it comes to moral behavior, we do not need to deny that the capacity for moral behavior has evolved along with developments in the evolution of the human brain. The content of any particular moral code differs between cultures. Even so, there is a strong argument put forward by some of the contributors to the symposium I mentioned, that underlines again the view proposed many years ago by C. S. Lewis that there does appear to be a thread running through all these different moral codes of what he called a universal law of right and wrong.

For those of us within the Hebrew-Christian tradition, our moral codes are informed by believing that God has spoken throughout the centuries through selected individuals and preeminently through Jesus Christ. In Jesus Christ we not only have detailed teaching about the moral code that should exemplify Christians but, what is much clearer and easier to understand, we see it embodied in a way that it has never been embodied in anyone, before or since, in the life that he lived and the death that he died. Actions speak much louder than words.

As far as I can see, it is not necessary to try to deny the emergence of elements of altruistic or self-giving behavior in nonhuman primates, for example, in order for us to affirm the reality of what we call *agap*e love. Agape love, we believe, was seen supremely and uniquely in the self-giving and self-emptying of Jesus Christ.

To many who claim to walk in the footsteps of Jesus Christ, the constant challenge remains to follow Christ's example and dedicate ourselves, seeking, however feebly, to embody in our lives more and more agape love.

11

What Is the Difference Between Altruism, Altruistic Love and Agape?

Malcolm,

Since altruism is observed in both animals and humans, why is it incorrect to conclude that, in this respect at least, we humans are nothing more than glorified animals? Doesn't it become a rather critical issue when altruism, in some of its forms, is held up in the Bible to be a salient feature of love for one's neighbor, one of the two great commandments?

Ben,

The altruism story is not new. When someone empathizes with another person's predicament, it often evokes a sympathetic feeling and altruistic acts. They are able to respond to what the other person is thinking and feeling. And that links in with mind reading, which we discussed earlier. To recap, according to my colleague Andrew Whiten, "Theory of mind refers to the everyday psychology that we use to understand and explain our own and others' actions by reference to mental states, such as 'knowing' and 'believing.'"[1] We humans seem to have an irresistible tendency to translate our understanding of the behavior of others into an assumption about their mental states. We represent to ourselves what people are doing in terms of what we believe they want, and what we believe they know and do not know, and, as we've seen before, it's this ability that has come to be known in cognitive science as "theory of mind."

The discovery of a possible brain mechanism for mind reading in primates forms a natural bridge between neuroscience, evolutionary psychology and social cognition.

The mind-reading story began twenty-five years ago when Giacomo Rizzolatti and his colleagues in Parma in Italy reported the discovery of neurons in the frontal lobes of the brains of monkeys that seemed to possess functional properties not previously observed.[2] The unusual property of these cells was that they were active not only when a monkey initiated a particular action, but also when the animal observed another monkey initiating or carrying out the same action. They labeled them "monkey see monkey do cells." These unusual neurons did not respond when the monkey was merely presented with a conventional visual stimulus. Rather, they were activated only when the monkey saw another individual (whether the human experimenter or another monkey) making a goal-directed action with a hand or mouth. One of Rizzolatti's collaborators, Vittorio Gallese, speculated that the primary role of these so-called mirror neurons was that they underlay the process of mind reading. This mirror neuron story is relevant to altruism since in recognizing someone else's distress we can read the other person's mind, empathize and act accordingly.

It now looks as if the behavior we see in humans, where one person helps another person in distress, is also evident in animals. Then, as you say, this worries some Christians because their non-Christian friends conclude that we are "nothing but" rather advanced animals. It is often assumed that our ability to empathize with someone else's predicament naturally evokes our altruistic response. Before the 1950s empathy used to be called "sympathy." Sympathy refers to one person feeling sorry for another, often as a result of perceiving the distress of the other subject. What has happened in the past half century is that the study of sympathy, as empathy, has been brought into the laboratory and into field studies of evolutionary psychologists. So today, striking anecdotal evidence is supplemented by controlled observation. The result: most researchers today believe that apes evaluate the emotional situations of others with a greater understanding than you find in most other animals, apart from ourselves.

The basic notion is not new. Charles Darwin suggested that empathy is something that exists to varying degrees in nonhuman species. Today, showing altruistic behavior, it is argued, implies a capacity for empathy, and this in turn depends on a capacity for mind reading, as a result of seeing the situation or predicament that the object is in. Cognitive empathy means that the emotional state arises because cognition helps interpret the distressing situation of the other. So, it is argued, showing altruistic behavior implies a capacity for empathy, and this in turn depends on a capacity for mind reading.

Today evolutionary psychologists and neuroscientists regard true empathy as a new, in evolutionary terms, cognitive skill. Looked at in this way, empathy becomes limited to animals or humans who can pass high-level cognitive tests, something that humans usually can do above a certain age.

The neuroscientific evidence is relevant, suggesting that many of these abilities are, at least in part, subserved by the prefrontal cortex, which, as Richard Byrne has shown, is an area in the neocortex of the brain that has expanded disproportionately in recent primate evolutionary history.

Further clues to the neural substrate of the ability to empathize come from the study of patients who have suffered damage to the prefrontal cortex and who show impairments in their ability to show empathy, usually labeled "sociopathy." There is clearly a social component to empathy. What it is, and how it works, is a problem, because the social world of primates is incredibly complex.

Malcolm,

So when altruism is looked at from an evolutionary perspective, it has come about through natural selection? But isn't there a problem with that, since the driving force for natural selection is survival of the fittest? So how did "altruistic" animals, who gave themselves up to save others, manage to pass on their genes? Surely that contradicts what we might predict from evolutionary theory?

Ben,

True, what looks like self-sacrificial behavior in animals, as well as humans, are examples of altruistic behavior. So how does evolutionary theory attempt to answer your question? First, it argues that genes favoring altruism can spread in future generations if their costs to the altruists' personal reproductive success is outweighed by the benefits in reproductive success of altruists' relatives carrying copies of the same genes—what is called "kin selection." Second, it proposes that genes favoring altruism could spread if the altruism is sufficiently reciprocated, what is called "reciprocal altruism."

Examples illustrating the first mechanism are widespread in the animal kingdom. Some of its most extreme forms are found, as one might expect, in those odd species where individuals of the colony are usually highly related to each other, such as social insects like bees and ants. One of the most graphic examples is honey-pot worker ants, who do nothing but hang from the ceiling of the ant colony, acting as receptacles or storage jars for honey, which some workers fill them with and which the colony draws on when needed. At an individual level, that is self-sacrifice! Examples of reciprocal altruism appear to be much rarer. Humans apart, there are only a handful of examples. A classic one is vampire bats, who are in real danger of starving if they fail to get their blood meal on a particular evening. If this happens they are fed back in their colony by an unrelated nest mate, to whom they are likely to repay the favor on another night.

These two examples necessitate a warning: we must not assume that because two behaviors are similar, the mechanisms underlying them are necessarily similar or identical. Leading evolutionary psychologist Frans de Waal has written helpfully about how to understand altruistic behaviors, as well as other kinds of behavior, that traditionally have been regarded as showing evidence of some sort of moral sense in an individual or group. In his book *Good Natured*, de Waal warns against unthinking reductionism. He cautions, "Even if animals other than ourselves act in ways tantamount to moral behavior, *their behavior does not necessarily rest on deliberations of the kind we engage in*. It is hard to believe that animals weigh their own interests against the rights of others, that they develop a vision of the greater good of society, or that they feel lifelong guilt about something they should not have done." And he goes on, "To communicate intentions and feelings is one thing; to clarify what is right, and why, and what is wrong, and why, is quite something else. Animals are no moral philosophers."[3] Of the moral sense, he later writes, "The fact that the human moral sense goes so far back in evolutionary history that other species show signs of it plants morality firmly near the center of our much-maligned nature."[4]

So the repeated take-home message is this: There is nothing remotely scientific about oversimplifying complex scientific issues in the interests of an ideological agenda. Unthinking reductionism can at times be a lazy response to avoid facing up to challenging scientific problems.

Most recently Professor Martin Nowak, theoretical biologist at Harvard, has published his first book for a popular audience titled *Super Cooperators.*[5] Nowak identifies five mechanisms, all found to some degree throughout the animal kingdom, that can make us work together. However, he adds, "no animal species can draw on the mechanisms to the same extent as seen in human society. Even our closest relatives, the apes, lack full-blown language and thus lack the full potential of indirect reciprocity."[6] And this is because, in indirect reciprocity, individuals benefit by taking into account the experiences of others. As such, it depends heavily on an ability to think abstractly enough to evaluate past behavior and to communicate. Nowak says that where there is direct and indirect reciprocity, his mathematical models show that the best approach is to be "hopeful, generous and forgiving." Surely the ingredients of altruism.

Malcolm,

The topic of reductionism seems to be coming up over and over again. I wonder if there are benefits in trying to go to a lower level in our attempts to understand behavior. For example, if we can find a clear genetic link with some particular patterns of behavior, that is very important. I thought such an approach was already reaping benefits in understanding the physical basis of things like autism and schizophrenia.

Ben,

A fair question. In the context of self-giving behavior, the evidence that points to a genetic component *influencing* the degree to which we show self-giving and self-limiting behavior must be placed firmly alongside the evidence that such behavior is not genetically *determined.* The way self-giving is expressed depends upon the moment-by-moment personal choices we make, which have a catalytic effect on our own behavior, and are also catalyzed by the degree of self-giving that we witness in the community we live in.

So while the evidence suggests that the rudiments of self-giving, self-limiting and self-sacrificing behavior are evident in nonhuman primates, at the same time constant vigilance is called for if we're to avoid slipping into sloppy thinking, assuming that similarities in overt behavior necessarily demonstrate identical underlying mechanisms to those behaviors.

Now back to your question about altruistic behavior, and how we should evaluate the evidence for it. More than a century ago a Bristol psychologist, Professor Lloyd Morgan, realized the potential pitfalls in explaining animal behavior *as if* the animals were humans. He believed we should always look for the simplest explanation. He suggested a rule that should guide us, now known as Lloyd Morgan's canon. It says, "In no case may we interpret an action as the outcome of a higher psychical faculty if it can be interpreted as the outcome of one which stands lower in the psychological scale."[7] In effect he is saying that there is at times a proper place for reductionism. The converse of this is an ever-present temptation to discuss animal behavior as if it is human. Frans de Waal warns, "The ultimate goal of the scientist is emphatically not to arrive at the most satisfactory projection of human feelings onto the animal, but rather at testable ideas and replicable observations. Thus anthropomorphisms serve the same exploratory function as that of intuition in all science, mathematics and medicine."[8] And as David Myers has documented, intuition has great powers but also some perils.[9]

But things are moving fast in this area of research. I have just been reading a paper in the Proceedings of the National Academy of Sciences in America published in June 2011 with the title "Evolutionary Foundations of Human Prosocial Sentiments." It is interesting that altruism is now being described as "human prosocial sentiments." The main thrust of this paper is that it is important to recognize that there may be fundamental differences in what motivates altruism across the primate order. And that raises the further question of how it was that we came as humans to be, as the paper puts it, "such unusual apes." The authors note that social relationships play an important role in the daily lives of both human and nonhuman primates. They help us to cope with chronic stresses of one sort or another. They are careful to note that "despite the intriguing parallels of the patterns of cooperation and correlates of social bonds among humans and other primates, there are also important differences in the scope of cooperation."[10] The important thing is that it should be possible, in quite a relaxed way, to engage in careful research into these differences.

There are no high stakes for the Christian in noting that altruism and mutual cooperation play important roles in the lives of nonhuman primates while at the same time remembering important differences in the scope of altruistic behavior between humans and other primates. One thing of interest is that in nonhuman primates altruism is strongly biased in favor of kin and reciprocating partners; it is never evident to strangers. A Christian is immediately reminded that we are called, as one of our top priorities, to be concerned with strangers. Another difference: unlike humans, nonhuman primates don't see any aversion to an inequitable distribution of the resources available that favor themselves. In other words, on the face of it, selfishness is quite acceptable—something that goes right against the grain of practical Christianity.

A Christian may be enthusiastically engaged, if that is their area of expertise, in research that deepens our knowledge of how altruistic behavior developed. At the same time, we should not be naive enough to pretend that the kind of altruistic behavior epitomized in the agape love at the heart of Christianity is just another version of altruistic behavior. Science does not progress by ignoring real differences where they exist. It wants to know the *why* behind these differences. What is their significance?

Malcolm,

Don't we have to think pretty carefully about the similarities and differences between altruism, altruistic love and the Christian notion of agape love? Can you help me to keep these distinctions clear?

Ben,

Altruism is what we might call having regard for the actions or motivations of others. *Altruistic love* normally adds an additional feature, a deep affirmative affect, to altruism. And *agape* is altruistic love extended to all humanity. But in addition to that, it has a very special use in the hands of the New Testament writers. There *agape* is the Greek word used to describe a form of unlimited altruistic love seen supremely in the self-giving of Christ on the cross. Up to a point it does have rough equivalents in Judaism and Buddhism and other great religious traditions. Ghandi, for example, in his teaching on nonviolence, talked about the universal law of love that he felt is present within human nature but can only be fully realized by those who "possess a living faith in the God of Love." Within the Jewish tradition the great physician Maimonides in his medieval oath said, "May the love for my art actuate me at all times; may neither avarice nor miserliness, nor thirst for glory or for a great reputation engage my mind . . . that I never see in a patient anything but a fellow creature in pain."

Within the Christian tradition the element of grace is a key feature of agape love. For example, the philosopher Charles Taylor wrote, "The original Christian notion of agape is the love that God has for humans which is connected with their goodness as creatures (though we don't have to decide whether they are loved because good or good because loved). Human beings participate through grace in this love. There is a divine affirmation of the creature, which is captured in the repeated phrase in Genesis 1 about each stage of creation, 'and God saw that it was good.' *Agape* is inseparable from such 'seeing good.'"[11]

In humans altruistic love is something we expect to see. It is almost ubiquitous in the parent-child relationship, implying no conscious benevolence on the part of the former. Holmes Ralston has suggested that in human evolution there is a critical new turning point—the capacity of altruistic acts and empathy, which are transposed into a new and higher key of human love and that the ideal of altruistic love is both established and practiced.[12]

Some philosophers such as Don Browning have argued that learning from the new insights into altruistic behavior from evolutionary psychology has prompted a rediscovery in some circles of the emphases brought out centuries ago by Thomas Aquinas. He had his own theory of kin altruism and kin preference. Aquinas thought that these contribute to our understanding of both parental and Christian love. As an example of the hints already evident in Aquinas's writing, we may note that in his *Summa Theologica* he wrote that humans love their children for two mutually reinforcing reasons: (1) because they are extensions of their own substance, and (2) because they mirror the goodness of God.[13] In effect, the approaches of biological functionalism and divine transcendence already coexisted in Aquinas's thought long before Charles Darwin. Frans de Waal also suggests that at times reciprocal altruism resembles features of self-sacrificial love as theologians would define it.

Perhaps there are lessons here for us all. As evolutionary psychologists we must be prepared to be agnostic or silent on metaphysical issues, and as Christians we should try to rid ourselves of the fear of naturalistic explanations of treasured aspects of our behavior. Both perspectives—the evolutionary psychological and that of Christian ethics—should keep their focus on the common ground between them without slipping into the error of inappropriately mixing their languages.

Malcolm,

I understand your point about the dangers of mixing our languages in an unthinking way. Now I have another question. Are we able to show altruism (and, in the Christian context, agape love) because of personality traits and inborn characteristics that each of us have inherited, or do we learn it as prosocial behavior? I've heard one of my lecturers say that some of the most intensively researched personality traits have been shown to have a genetic component.

Ben,

When reviewing the literature on this recently, Michael McCullough concluded that the most predominant theme that arose from the existing research literature was the clear evidence that altruistic behavior is multiply determined.[14] Knowledge of personality characteristics provides the building blocks on which altruism is based, but these characteristics combine with all sorts of things like gender, culture and religion, that in turn affect the general learning inclination to behave in altruistic ways.

Research has shown that personality traits that are thought to facilitate altruism differ depending upon whether the altruism is directed toward kin or nonkin. In this context the social psychologists call altruism "prosocial behavior" and find that we show prosocial behavior toward close relationship partners (our kin) or toward people in general (nonkin). These two forms of behavior are related to some similar personality substrates and some that are different.

One study that addressed the question of a possible genetic component as to whether someone showed altruistic behavior involved the participation of 839 twin pairs—509 were identical twins, and 330 were fraternal twins. One of their conclusions was that the variation in the likelihood of showing what they called "affective empathy" seemed to have a considerable genetic component.[15]

In another study, researchers analyzed the results of 172 earlier studies investigating any links between gender and the likelihood of showing helping behavior. They concluded, "Results from our meta-analytic review of sex differences in helping behavior indicate that in general men helped more than women and women receive more help than men."[16] (I wonder if you find this counterintuitive as I do? But this may just be an example of where my own natural intuition is wrong.)

Another extensive study investigating how personality correlates with the giving of help, the receiving of help and the importance of helping collected data in six different countries in the world. One of their conclusions was that "sex differences are present for the altruism scale as a whole, with almost all the differences showing males to be more altruistic."[17]

Another study, this time looking at more than five hundred pairs of identical and nonidentical twins, some of whom were male and some who were female, found that the women had higher scores than men on altruism. Overall this study confirmed that there was a strong heritability component for the measures of altruism that they used and this applied to both men and women.[18]

Yet another study shows the complexity of the research situation in seeking further knowledge on some of these issues. A study that looked at ten separate personality variables and how these were linked to the likelihood of showing prosocial behavior concluded that whether a relationship exists depends on the type of situation in question. It also concluded that identical personality traits do not generally operate in similar ways in males and females. All this warns against the danger of making wide generalizations on this issue. We might easily get so preoccupied with the possible genetic components to the expression of altruistic behavior as to ignore the extent to which a person's current situation and social class also influence the likelihood of showing altruistic behavior. Both of these factors were shown to affect the likelihood of acting altruistically.[19]

I hope you are not wishing now that you had never asked this question because I've gone on far too long. I do think it was an important question and one that could be worrying to some Christians. It goes back again to the question of whether each individual's capacity for behaving in a Christian way is dependent upon their inherited characteristics, and if so, to what extent. My own view is that from a Christian perspective there are no grounds for believing that we are all created identical in terms of things like personality. Indeed, the apostle Paul makes it clear that we are in fact all very different and we have many different gifts. I was reminded recently when reading some of the things that the apostle Paul had to say to the Christians at Corinth about the way that some of them were boasting about themselves and their behavior. Paul said that by the standards of the world, the Corinthians may have had something of which to boast, but that Christians do not accept the standards of the world. Christians acknowledge that in themselves they are nothing. They owe everything to the grace of God and there is no place at all for boasting about one's achievements. As Christians we acknowledge that we are all different, and it is the grace of God that enables us, in the context of the individual differences, to show agape love as much as we are able.

12

Does Language Uniquely Define Us as Humans?

Malcolm,

While we are discussing animal/human similarities and differences, can I ask about something that came up in this week's lectures? We were told about the evidence from the last half century's research on what some people have called "language" in animals. The lecturer told us the usual stuff about the language of the bees, and then described attempts over the last thirty or forty years to teach chimpanzees to use symbols. Apparently, they can put symbols together to form what are often regarded as sentences in order to ask for things that they want. Does this mean that another key feature of humans—namely, language—can no longer be regarded as unique to humans?

Ben,

You are taking some busy and demanding classes! New work emerges all the time in an attempt to study the rudiments of language in nonhuman primates. Here again I am fortunate in having one of the active researchers in this field as a colleague in St Andrews—more of that in a moment.

It's true there have been many attempts to teach animals human language, but most of them have proved to be a dead end. There is no doubt that animals can communicate expressively. (Any dog owner knows how their dog can make his desires known, but dogs will never link symbolic sounds together in sentences or have anything close to language.) But trying to teach a language to chimpanzees and other species has a long history, and puzzles remain. In the past century there was a series of such attempts. Two of these projects took infant chimpanzees into researchers' own homes, where the researchers treated them as they treated their own children. The young apes showed their intelligence in many ways but not linguistically. In light of today's knowledge, this is not surprising since we now know that chimpanzees lack fine motor control of their voices and can't imitate any new sounds.

Subsequent projects used the gestural system of American sign language. All these projects were to an extent successful: chimpanzees learned and used American sign language gestures and were able to respond appropriately to questions posed using visual symbols. One project that got a lot of attention was with Kanzi, who, like children, picked up his knowledge of a language without being taught. He recognized some spoken English words and remarkably seemed to understand some syntactical rules. It became clear, first, that language may exist in the absence of speech; and second, that Kanzi was in fact not a chimpanzee as was previously thought, but a bonobo.[1]

Today the focus is much more on the recognition that humans evolved through a phase in which their language was gestural and not spoken. This approach is supported by the intricate relationship that we are now aware of between the neural substrates of human language and manual skills—something shown by similar damage causing both apraxias and aphasias in humans. Surprisingly research on great ape gestural communication has been sparse. Today almost all the work on this topic comes from only two research groups, the team in Leipzig in Germany and the team here in St Andrews.

Recently my colleague Klaus Zuberbuhler has argued that what is missing is an intention to communicate, noting that children from the youngest ages have a great desire to share information with others, even though they gain no immediate benefit in doing so. That seems not to be the case with other primates.

Klaus comments, "In principle, the chimp could produce all the sounds a human produces but they don't do so because there has been no evolutionary pressure in this direction, there is nothing to talk about for a chimp because he has no interest in talking about it."[2] He believes that at some point in human evolution, people developed the desire to share thoughts, and when that happened, the underlying systems of perceiving and producing sounds were already in place as part of the primate heritage, and natural selection had only to find a way of connecting these systems of thought.

Klaus adds, "Please keep in mind that we recently had to revise this position somewhat following a study carried out with the Budongo chimps. In this recent study, the main finding was that chimps occasionally do inform others, provided the event is highly relevant and provided the recipients are ignorant of the event. We are currently analyzing the results of two more experiments of this type, so a more complete story is likely to emerge in the near future."[3] All this should serve as a reminder of how fast research is moving in this field and a further warning not to rush to conclusions when you read headline-grabbing media reports of research in this area of science.

Malcolm,

I find this topic fascinating. I am curious, however, about the point of all this kind of research looking for the similarities and differences in things like language between humans and animals. What are your thoughts?

Ben,

Well I suppose that the first answer to your question is that if we understood the origins of language, it would help also in understanding the emergence of our human capacities for reflection, rationality and deliberation, including ethical decision making, and in moving forward into the future.

I think a second way of answering that question was brought out very nicely in a 2006 report of a working group of the Academy of Medical Sciences in Britain, "The Use of Nonhuman Primates in Research."[4] Let me illustrate with a few quotes. They said, "Researchers attested that many important discoveries about how the brain works in both health and disease stem from studies using non-human primates. While these findings complement and extend findings derived from other approaches, it was claimed that in many cases *they could not have been obtained by other means*."[5]

Here are a few other quotes that I think illustrate the major point of the potential benefit of such research on animals to human health and wellbeing. They wrote, "Primates, both human and non-human, embody a major evolutionary step-change in vertebrate brain architecture with the massive expansion of the neocortex. . . . Only the non-human primate brain has a cellular composition of divisions that is in any way directly analogous to that found in humans."[6]

Comments like these also alert us to the need not to make sweeping statements about similarities between animals and humans that are not only misleading but simply untrue. The same report quotes a point regarding discussions of intelligence: "A recent review of the evolution of intelligence places more emphasis on the continuity of humans with other primates: '*The outstanding intelligence of humans appears to result from a combination and enhancement of properties found in non-human primates, such as theory of mind, imitation and language, rather than from "unique" properties.*'"[7]

13

Does My Brain Have a "God Spot"?

Malcolm,

I've been thinking about something I heard in passing in a recent lecture. The lecturer, in talking about how things like recognizing faces and understanding language are localized in the brain, mentioned that there had been recent claims that a "God spot" has been discovered in the brain. Is this true? And does this discovery explain away belief in the existence of God?

Ben,

You are not alone in asking whether rapid developments in what is called "neurotheology" can help to prove the existence of God. You could ask, Is the discovery of the "God spot" analogous to the discovery of endorphin receptors, which, for neuroscientists, implied the existence of endorphins, which were later discovered?

A book by Carol Albright and James Ashbrook titled *Where God Lives in the Human Brain,* which I think I mentioned briefly early on in our correspondence, prompted widespread interest in attempts to link the brain with religious experience.[1] It was widely discussed and gave a fresh impetus in the search for the so-called God module in the brain. This module, some people claim, is the neural substrate making possible our spirituality—in my view, an unjustifiable claim. Looking ahead a bit, I say this because I think that the biblical portraits of the human person, in holistic terms, resonate with and underline the portraits emerging from science that emphasize that the whole person—brain, body, mind and feelings—makes true spirituality possible.

I think that past discussions of brain and spirituality help us here. Many who have written on the topic have begun with the apostle Paul's experience on the Damascus road. They speculate that Paul was an epileptic. Then they quickly move on to assume that Paul's religiosity was that of a typical epileptic patient.

In 1838 Esquirol recognized an apparent association between religiosity and epilepsy. Two millennia earlier, Hippocrates, the father of medicine, had called epilepsy "the sacred disease." More recent studies have shown that the so-called hyper-religiosity of some epileptics is not always a feature of individuals with temporal lobe epilepsy. Moreover, although hyper-religiosity and temporal lobe epilepsy do occur in some individuals, there does not appear to be a direct causal relationship between repeated seizure discharge of the temporal lobes and hyper-religiosity. The lack of this clear link has, however, not prevented people from continuing to link religious experience generally, and religious awareness in particular, with the selective activity of certain parts of the brain.

There is a long history of similar attempts to link bodily processes and spirituality. Almost two centuries ago, when phrenology was as popular as neurotheology is today, thoughtful Christians were trying to answer questions about how they could relate the then available knowledge about localization of function in the brain with spirituality.

If you happen to have read a recent bestseller by Mary Ann Shaffer and Annie Barrows, titled *The Guernsey Literary and Potato Peel Pie Society*, you may remember the wonderful episode when one of the members of the Guernsey Literary Society is sent a book published in the mid-1800s with the wonderful title *The New Illustrated Self-Instructor in Phrenology and Psychiatry: with Size and Shape Tables and Over One-Hundred Illustrations*. The subtitle is *Phrenology: the Science of Interpreting Bumps on the Head*.

You may also remember that Isola, the overenthusiastic recipient of this book, promptly starts to measure the heads of all of her friends, looking for bumps that will tell her what their major personality characteristics are. She tells the rector of her local church that she will no longer need to dress up as a fortuneteller and read palms at the annual harvest festival gathering but now she will read bumps instead. Isola becomes so enthusiastic that she describes this new science of phrenology as "a real lightning bolt," saying that "I've found out more in the last three days than I knew in my whole life before."[2] Sadly this tremendous enthusiasm eventually totally evaporates as Isola discovers that what the bumps tell her about all these people she knows so well, and has lived with for so long, does not fit at all with the experience and evidence gathered over many decades. As she puts it, eventually she has to abandon it all in light of the real facts. Such is life! As the Oxford theologian Austin Farrer wrote many years ago, "Reality is a nuisance to those who want to make it up as they go along."[3]

Malcolm,

Are you saying that you don't deny that there may be an explanation for things like praying and meditating in terms of what is happening in the brain? Does that mean that God, religion and spirituality are now known to be nothing but brain processes?

Ben,

I'm sorry if I have confused you. I was really trying to say that just as some people used the well-documented history of phrenology, which claimed to provide scientific evidence of spiritual bumps on the brain surface, as an explanation of religious behavior and experience, so today neurotheology has been used by some to try and prove the reality of spiritual things. But the question remains: What happens if, just as phrenology was shown to be wrong and an unsure foundation for grounding religious beliefs, today's neurotheology is later shown to be wrong? Indeed some of the early claims by high-profile figures in the field, like Michael Persinger, are already appearing simplistic in light of more recent research.[4] Two recent papers show how views about the link between spirituality and the brain are changing.

In 2005 Kevin Seybold wrote a paper with the title "God and the Brain: Neuroscience Looks at Religion."[5] The article reviews "the role of the brain in experiencing God, and the question of the innateness of spirituality."

Seybold notes how some of the earliest work by Michael Persinger focused primarily on the role of the temporal lobe structures in normal religious and mystical experience. According to Persinger's hypothesis, religious experience is caused by short-term, localized electrical activity within the temporal lobe known as temporal lobe transients. Persinger claims that we have experiences of God because the temporal lobes developed evolutionarily the way they did. Had the structures within the temporal lobe developed differently, according to Persinger, the God experience would not have occurred. Seybold criticizes Persinger's tendency to mix his languages, writing, "Indeed, some scientists studying brain and religion have made philosophical statements disguised as science, or have resorted to ontological reductionism in their analysis of experimental data."

Other authors argue for the importance of the limbic structures for providing the foundation for spiritual and religious experience. A more balanced approach by Saver and Rabin reminds us, "Religious experience involves the same brain areas as non-religious experience with the exception that religious experiences that are particularly ineffable and profound are made such by the involvement of the limbic system which 'marks' the experience as depersonalized, critically important, or ecstatic and joyful."[6]

What Seybold describes as "perhaps the most celebrated research on the neural basis of religious experience," that of Andrew Newberg, brought the literature to a broader public awareness. There were other attempts to argue for the evolution and development of the parts of the brain responsible for spirituality. But, as Seybold points out, all this begs the question that if, for example, Sigmund Freud was correct that religious beliefs were all an illusion, why would it be beneficial to humans to develop brains enabling them to indulge in illusionary thoughts and beliefs? How would this aid survival? The converse of this argument is that if God exists and has created humans so that they may enjoy a relationship with him, it is not surprising that there is a physical mechanism that makes possible development of that relationship.

Now fast forward to 2009, when a review paper by Alexander Fingelkurts and Andrew Fingelkurts appears in the journal *Cognitive Processing* with the title "Is Our Brain Hardwired to Produce God, or Is Our Brain Hardwired to Perceive God? A Systematic Review on the Role of the Brain in Mediating Religious Experience."[7] The paper by Seybold was eight pages long and had forty references. This paper is forty pages long and has four hundred references—an indication of how fast this field of research is developing.

In light of the Fingelkurts's paper, Persinger's claim that religion is located in the temporal lobes seems overly simplistic. The authors identified, from the studies so far reported, more than forty distinct regions of the brain that had been shown to be selectively active in different religious activities such as praying and meditating. So the idea of a "God spot" is so simplistic as to be not worth pursuing. At another level of investigation the authors also review the evidence for the part played by neuro mediating systems in religious experience. These include dopaminergic systems, acetylcholinergic, serotoninergic and glutaminergic systems, which you will have heard about in your courses.

So the Fingelkurts's review demonstrates dramatically just how rapidly the field is moving and how complex is the whole issue of seeking to relate aspects of religious experience and spirituality to specific localized regions of the brain. And yet even this excellent review at times betrays what looks like a desire somehow to use science to bring God back into the equation when it says, "There might be room for divine influences in biological evolution."

You will be very well aware that this is an attempt to sneak in the God-of-the-gaps approach to the relation between science and religion by the back door. Why do you need "room" if God is there already upholding all things?

Kevin Seybold was more careful to avoid a reductionist approach and to be humble about how little we really know about the brain. His article concludes by recognizing the importance of bringing a "levels of explanation" perspective to the study of religious experience.

Malcolm,

I'm intrigued by what you said about God and the brain. I had a course on brain structures and functions as part of the neuropsychology studies, so I'd be interested in hearing more details about the conclusions of the long paper you mentioned.

Ben,

I didn't want to overload you with details, but I'm happy to do this.

The major conclusions of the paper by Alexander Fingelkurts and Andrew Fingelkurts are:

1. "Religious experience does not involve a specific neural system and probably requires joint activation of a family of systems, each of which is usually involved in nonreligious contexts."[8]
2. "A detailed analysis of the literature has revealed no consistent hemispheric prevalence of one particular brain area during religious experience."[9]
3. "In spite of almost fifty years of EEG studies of religious experience, no clear consensus about the underlying neuro physiologic substrate of religious experience has emerged."[10]
4. "All the main neuromediator systems in the brain are involved (except the noradrenalergic system) in religious experience."[11]
5. "At the moment neuroscience can not provide a reliable explanation for religious experience. However, already today cognitive neuroscience, in a broad sense, may contribute to an overall description of religious experience with regard to biological and psychological dimensions."[12]

These conclusions taken seriously may help modern-day neurotheology to avoid erroneously following in phrenology's footsteps. No one doubts the massive empirical data that has been collected relating brain activity and various measures of religiosity. The question is whether investigations of the relationship between brain activity and religious/spiritual activity have always been scientific. While many neurotheological investigations would only claim to be exploratory, some purport to be experimental in nature. But are these empirical data just collected in support of specific hypotheses? One must ask whether the investigations are conducted in a manner that could, in principle, disprove the hypotheses. As was true for phrenology, there will be problems if investigations are designed only to collect confirming evidence or if results are explained in a post hoc manner.

Careful researchers like the neuroradiologist Andrew Newberg, who secured the cooperation of Tibetan monks and Franciscan nuns who agreed to have their brains monitored while they were meditating, usually avoid using the results of their studies to produce some sort of argument for the existence of God. Occasionally, however, even they seem to want to extend their claims. For example, Newberg and Waldman wrote, "So wherever you turn, or whomever you ask, it appears as though everyone has some image of God, even if represented by nothing other than a blank sheet of paper. To a neuroscientist this suggests that believers and disbelievers may harbour a 'God neuron' or 'God circuit' somewhere inside the brain."[13] This unfortunately easily becomes a rather unsubtle mixing of the methods and language of science and religion and becomes a veiled attempt to confer the popularly perceived authority of science upon that of religion. But as you have discovered now in your neuropsychology lectures, it is a reasonable extrapolation, on current evidence, to say that everything that happens in the mind has its brain correlates.

Overall, I believe Andrew Newberg is pursuing important research while recognizing that occasionally he slips into referring to "God neurons." His research is important because we need to recognize that there are forms of distressing psychiatric illnesses which, among other things, present themselves as bizarre religious beliefs and feelings. Newberg's research has the potential to reveal clues to the neurological substrates of some of these bizarre ideas and then to work towards a possible neuropharmacological course of relieving the distressing symptoms of the suffering person.

There is also often confusion in discussions of how "real" these religious experiences are. They are all "real" if by real we mean observable changes in the flux of electrons along neurons and the flow of neurotransmitters at synapses. After all, you can observe similar changes in brain activity when a person takes a hallucinogen such as peyote, long used by some Native Americans in their religious rituals. If you stick strictly to what is happening in the head, the use of words like *real* and *illusory* becomes meaningless. And in any case, why should you elevate one unusual religious experience and try to give it pride of place among all the others? God may be encountered equally through reason as through ecstasy, as much through morning prayer in the Anglican tradition as through clapping and dancing in the Pentecostal tradition.

While this sort of research in neurotheology makes fascinating reading, and it's easy, in some ways, to dismiss it, nevertheless I think that it is potentially an important new research area that can and should be done, providing it is done in a genuine spirit of scientific exploration and not as a means to prop up beliefs held on other grounds. The reason it is potentially important is that any practicing psychiatrist will tell you how, at times, a person's illness may present itself in terms of bizarre religious feelings, experiences and beliefs. These all have their neural and biochemical substrates, and if it is possible to learn more about these, it may be possible to develop psychotropic drugs to help relieve such distressing conditions in addition, as appropriate, to any course of psychotherapy.

Malcolm,

I see why people are trying to link religious experience with brain activity, but I still don't see why this doesn't just reduce religious experience to "nothing but" brain activity. Doesn't it empty religious beliefs of any claims to be saying something important and of lasting truth?

Ben,

I agree that it is extremely easy to slip into a criticism of religion, calling into question the reality of religious experience, on the grounds that it is "nothing but" the activity of particular parts of the brain. But a similar claim could be made about the mental processes involved in putting together and presenting the case against the reality of religious beliefs and experiences, that they are "nothing but" the mindless chattering of certain pathways in the brain. In a word, it is a self-defeating argument. That is not to say that, as I mentioned, some forms of religious experience may be artificially induced by, for example, the use of hallucinogenic drugs, while others result from reflecting upon the Creator and the beauty and wonder of the created order, or being carried away while listening to Verdi's *Requiem*.

Malcolm,

This raises another question for me: How are we to understand the reports in the Bible, for example, of visions and trances? What makes religious experience religious?

Ben,

As I said before, it is hard to imagine someone taking the view that religiosity could occur without some accompanying brain activity. What kinds of possible relationships might exist between brain and spiritual activities? The answer would appear to depend on how we define and then operationalize our terms. Defining what we mean by "brain activity" may not be a problem. Once we decide on the level we wish to examine (i.e., neurochemical or single-cell recording or patterns of blood flow), we would then choose an established procedure for making measurements. Most would agree that spiritual activity is the more difficult part of the relationship to define and measure. Many neurotheological investigations have examined what they call "extraordinary" aspects of spiritual activity such as visions or trances or ecstasies. More mundane aspects, such as reading and thinking about the Scriptures or participating in a worship service, have received less attention. Perhaps there is already an assumption that these more mundane activities are subserved by the same brain systems that will be active when we read or think about nonholy writings or participate in nonreligious social activities. The "extraordinary" activities, on the other hand, might be supposed to involve unique brain circuits. Such a distinction would need to be justified. As of today I know of no satisfying justification that has been put forward.

And then of course there are activities that might not even be considered "spiritual" by some people, though in the Christian tradition are certainly considered to be so. I have in mind activities such as feeding the poor, caring for the sick and visiting the prisoners. Miroslav Volf—who has been described by Rowan Williams, the Archbishop of Canterbury, as "one of the most celebrated theologians of our day"—has written, "Some people like to keep their spirituality and theology neatly separated, the way someone may want to have the main dish and the salad served separately during a meal. I don't. Spirituality that's not theological will grope in the darkness, and theology that's not spiritual will be emptied of its most important content."[14]

Malcolm,

I've never really thought much about what is usually meant by *spiritual.* Among the people I know, it is just assumed that we all know what we're talking about, but I suppose that since we claim to take the Bible seriously we should base our meaning and use of the word *spiritual* on what the Bible has to say about it.

Ben,

There is an ongoing debate about whether spiritual activity should be regarded as a way of perceiving, a way of experiencing or a way of behaving.

Most researchers seem to define spirituality or religiosity in terms of how we interpret the world in affective terms. Overall I think it is now more widely recognized that religious/spiritual behavior must be understood in terms of emotion, perception, self-consciousness, memory and many other functions. Thus the relationship between brain activity and religious/spiritual behavior may be diffuse and context dependent; too much so, in fact, to build a convincing simplistic neurotheology.

As a footnote, let me add a cautionary word about claims that we know exactly how brain pictures using MRI are to be interpreted. This caution is not of my own making, but from specialists in the techniques for brain imaging. Despite occasional warnings from scientists using MRI and working at the leading edge of research, results have at times been reported in the media and popular press that look like a return to the outmoded phrenology of the nineteenth century.

In mid-2010, a paper claimed that some MRI sequences might in fact change mood and treat depression. Mark George, the author of this recent report, concludes,

> This paper has enormous implications for safety and for potentially creating a new generation of combined stimulators/scanners. In terms of safety we can no longer assume that MRI does not affect the brain. There needs to be a broad re-examination of which field strengths and gradient switching protocols are safe and which are not. This study suggests that, if one could better understand how the MRI causes changes in metabolism, one could create the machines of the future, where one could scan in one instance and stimulate the other, all with the same device.[15]

All this is exciting but also a very salutary warning. The importance of all this is not that earlier findings using MRI have to be discarded, but that when using MRI it is not simply a matter of identifying changes in brain activity; MRI does itself produce changes in brain metabolism.

Malcolm,

If some brain processes are associated with spiritual activity, can we use this to "prove" that there is a God? Meaning, can we argue that since we have brains that enable us to respond to God in prayer and meditation, there must be a God who made us this way? So it "explains" why we believe?

Ben,

I'm a keen fly fisherman, so let me use an analogy from my favorite sport to see if it helps to clarify why I don't think that demonstrating that there are brain processes associated with particular activities can be used to prove the existence of things, and that making inferences from brain states can become a risky business.

Sir Henry Wotton, referred to in the classic book *The Complete Angler*, describes fishing as "a rest to his mind, the cheerer of his spirits, the diverter of sadness, the calmer of unquiet thoughts, the moderator of passions, a procurer of contentedness."[16] Such a description might suggest a brain state similar to some forms of religious meditation. But, says Sir Henry, it comes when he is enjoying fly fishing. I know the feeling!

Let us imagine that we could study Sir Henry's brain with modern fMRI techniques while he is fishing. Imagine we find certain brain areas are more active than others. Suppose we do the same experiment with half a dozen more fly fishermen like me, and behold, the same areas become active in each of our brains! So have we discovered the brain areas for fishing? And does the observation that the same area lights up in all of us prove the existence of fish? Either the fish are there in the river or they are not. Casting a fly over them and observing that a particular part of our brains lights up won't prove they exist. Brain imaging alone is not going to provide unequivocal evidence for or against the existence and action of God.

The logic is the same when we study the brains of people engaged in spiritual activities or the brain correlates of atheism. That certain brain areas light up can never prove the existence of the God on whom the spiritual activities are focused. Either God exists or he does not. As Christians we differ in how we became Christians, how we practice our faith and so on, and likewise (for a variety of different reasons) we believe that God exists. And the weight that each of us accords to these different reasons will vary from person to person. Some Christians have seen what personal belief in Jesus Christ has done for a friend. Others have studied the Scriptures with an open mind and become convinced of the claims of Jesus Christ, and responded to his invitation to come to him, to put their trust in him. Others have come in other ways. You only have to look at the records of the lives of the early church and of the early Christian disciples in the

Acts of the Apostles to see the variety of ways in which people became Christians.

Ultimately appealing to subjective experiences alone as the grounds for beliefs is an unsure and moving foundation. It was certainly never one used by the early Christians. If you read the accounts given in the New Testament, for example, you will find that the constant grounds appealed to for taking seriously the claims of Jesus Christ are not subjective feelings in times of ecstasy, but the many and varied accounts of the life, teaching and activities of Jesus and his disciples.

In other words, for those who are willing to examine the evidence with an open and critical mind, the evidence—or perhaps better, the testimony—is open and available. It's important to say that it is open and available, and does not require any presuppositions, although many agree that there is more evidence for the existence and the life of Jesus Christ than for other historical figures around the same time that most people take for granted, such as Julius Caesar. As Oxford historian Diarmaid MacCulloch wrote recently in his 1161-page magisterial volume *Christianity: The First Three Thousand Years,* "There is, however, an important aspect of Christianity on which it is the occupation of historians to speak: the *story* of Christianity is undeniably true, in that it is part of human history."[17] Ultimately, however, at no point, as far as I can see, is the claim made that people are to be argued into the kingdom of God. Rather the main thrust of the message is that Jesus Christ is alive and offers the opportunity of entering into a personal relationship with him.

14

Does God Guide and Direct Us?

Malcolm,

I've been thinking about how our conscious choices and social influences interact with what is happening in our brains as we seek God's guidance.

You remember I told you about some talks at my local church about the Christian mind. Our next series focused on the use of our minds in seeking guidance, which prompted me to question some of the things that were said about dramatic examples of how God spoke to people directly, while others seem to be guided through very mundane everyday circumstances.

How do you acknowledge the diversity of views about how Christians get guidance from God for life's choices? How much involves using the mind? How much depends on feelings and emotions? What about hearing voices and seeing visions?

Ben,

What a huge topic. I shall confine my comments to one or two aspects of guidance where I think recent developments in cognitive neuroscience may help a bit in disentangling some of the relevant factors at work in seeking God's guidance.

First, yes there are episodes in Scripture where dramatic guidance is given. For example, an inner voice at Saul's conversion, Matthew's calling to follow Jesus and so on. But as far as I can see, nowhere in Scripture are we encouraged to see these as the norm. That makes good sense. Hearing voices and seeing visions can be strong pointers to psychopathology, and with suitable drug treatment the visions disappear and the voices can be cured.

Second, neuroscience makes it clear that the strict separation of mind and feeling or emotion is not the way we are made. Neurologist Antonio Damasio has done in-depth studies of individuals with injury to the orbital frontal cortex of the brain. After his research, he developed a so-called theory of somatic markers of the relation of what goes wrong in this sort of brain injury. He explored this in detail in his book *Descartes' Error: Emotion, Reason and the Human Brain.*[1] According to this theory, our life experiences help our minds develop automatic responses to events. These are coupled with our knowledge of the world. At moments when our consciousness lacks the relevant knowledge for a decision, we are guided by subtle emotions and intuitions. These might include feeling suspicions toward a person or feeling that a certain behavior might not be the right thing to do. In many circumstances these autonomic responses guide our behavior.

The implication of Damasio's theory is that emotions deliver many of our most complex and rational judgments about the world, guiding us in our moment-to-moment decision making. Without knowing why, we often just feel that this or that is the right thing to do.

I only mention this as an example of the artificiality of thinking we can totally disconnect mind and emotion. That's not the way we are made. That is not the way the brain works. The question remains how to keep a proper balance. There are no simple answers as far as I can see from within neuropsychology.

Third, I think that we need to learn from the wisdom of the past, from long before we had our current knowledge about how the brain works and how mind and emotion are so intimately interconnected. Peter Enns, for example, emphasizes, "It is important for future generations of Christians to have a view of the Bible where its rootedness in ancient ways of thinking is embraced as a theological positive, not a problem to be overcome."[2] He adds that "Christians can turn away, but the current scientific explanation of cosmic and biological origins is not going away, nor is our growing understanding of the nature of Israelite faith in its ancient Near Eastern context."[3]

At this point I find it useful to stop and remember that in Scripture there is a strong encouragement to engage our minds, our rational thinking ability. You remember we began by talking about the great scientist Robert Boyle and how he urges us to develop an "examined faith"—a place where our minds are fully engaged. Long before that, the apostle Paul urged us to have a "reasonable" or "reasoning" faith (Acts 18:4; Romans 12:2).

I also believe that too often we fail to learn from wiser Christians of former generations such as Saint Ignatius, who had much of importance to say about guidance. He reminded us that, at times, a careful and deliberative process must be involved. It includes weighing up certainties and doubts, consolations (things that seem to draw us closer to Jesus) and desolations (what seems to draw us away from Jesus), what attracts and appeals, what seems to be highlighted and what isn't. In this way, gradually, we sense God's calling and we make a choice. This is Saint Ignatius's preferred way. Keep the mind fully engaged and then, because of how we are made, our emotions will play their proper part.

Finally, there's all the work on social neuroscience we have just been discussing, part of the leading-edge work today, where we are constantly reminded of the key importance of social interaction in our cognitive processes, our neural processes and our decision making, and hence in guidance.

This, as you well know, resonates with pervasive biblical themes about the importance of membership in the community of faith. The Hebrews knew it so well, and the New Testament takes up this emphasis by reminding Christians repeatedly that they are members of the body of Christ. We are all members of one body, but we are all distinctive individuals with different gifts. Membership in the church community of believers is not an optional extra for the Christian who happens to like making friends and being with other people. Being a member of the community of the church is part of who and what we are.

We wrote a few years ago about the relevance of social psychology for Christian faith: "It is the whole believing people, not isolated believers, that is the body of Christ. To say the church is Christ's body reminds us that together we can admonish one another. Together we can enable each other to minister."[4]

And in the context of our present discussion I would add that it is together that we can be guided as, in love, we give frank advice to our fellow Christians who face choice points in their lives requiring, at times, difficult decisions. It is so easy to deceive ourselves with wishful thinking that we need to test our thoughts against the sounding board of fellow believers. They may bring a wider perspective on an issue with which we have become so preoccupied that it has grown out of all proper perspective.

15

Does Neuropsychology Have Anything to Offer Psychotherapy and Counseling?

Malcolm,

We have just started six lectures on psychotherapy and clinical psychology. The lecturer has emphasized that all she is doing in this very short course is to make us aware of one of the areas of contemporary psychology in which the largest number of trained psychologists are employed today.

I remember you saying some time ago that in America the majority of psychologists who are Christians tend to become clinical psychologists, counselors or psychotherapists because they see this as a way of fulfilling their Christian calling to help those in need. Remembering how much time we have spent in discussing the very rapid developments in neuropsychology led me to wonder whether the neuroscience and neuropsychological parts of psychology are relevant to those other specialized fields. Since clinical psychology and psychotherapy focus so much on situations where there is serious mental distress or tensions in interpersonal relations, do the advances in cognitive neuroscience have any relevance here?

Ben,

You have an uncanny knack for posing what look like relatively simple and straightforward questions but which, on reflection, implicitly raise profound issues that have been around for a very long time. Your mention of your lecturer's reference to clinical psychology, psychotherapy, counseling and so on brings to mind a lively debate that has been going on for more than a century among psychologists who are Christians, about whether there is such a thing as "Christian psychology."

You are fortunate. I notice that InterVarsity Press has just published a second edition of a book titled *Psychology and Christianity: Five Views*.[1] I suggest you get ahold of it. It will give you a good introduction to the ongoing debates among people who have shared Christian convictions, but differ over questions such as whether there is such a thing as "Christian psychology," "Christian counseling" or "Christian psychotherapy." One of the contributors to this book, David Myers, represents the view that I would take on these issues. He calls it a Levels-of-Explanation View. I think it's a useful book because each of the contributors is able to put forward their view, and the other contributors can then respond from their particular standpoint. In this way it is a model of the open-minded debates that Christians, with shared Christian convictions, should have on contentious issues at the science and faith interfaces.

I was trained initially as a natural scientist, so for me the whole idea of there being such a thing as a "Christian psychology" seems bizarre. When I was studying physics and chemistry, for example, I never thought that there were things called "Christian physics" or "Christian chemistry." Having said that, and being mindful of the very profound insights into human nature with which the Bible is replete, I can well understand how some people would wish to regard it as being full of psychology. But you have to be careful what you mean by that. I suppose you could say that the Bible is full of astronomy, with its references to the sun rising and the sun setting, and yet I doubt anyone would want to suggest that there is such a thing as a "Christian astronomy" because it's so obvious that astronomical science is a totally different venture from astronomical references in the Bible. I think that in general the same applies to psychology, at least as it is conceived today.

Malcolm,

Given what you say about there not being "Christian psychology" any more than there is a "Christian physics" or "Christian chemistry," how do you avoid developing a divided mind that can't honestly deal with the implications of your Christian faith for your psychology and of your psychology for your Christian beliefs?

Ben,

Any claim to talk about the integration of psychology and Christian belief must, I believe, deal with psychology as it actually is today. It is not satisfactory to attempt to confine one's discussion of psychology to some small section of it—for example, focusing exclusively on personality or counseling—and in so doing to fail to take account of the vast majority of the psychological landscape as it is today. We've already seen that psychology has very strong links with neuroscience and cognitive science, and that must be kept in mind. It remains the case, as I said a moment ago, that when you come to topics like clinical psychology, including personality theory, these questions about how properly to relate one's personal beliefs, including religious beliefs, loom large. If you are dealing with aspects of contemporary psychology that express their models in mathematical equations, such as visual perceptual psychology, it is difficult to see how you could "integrate" Christianity and psychology. I find it very difficult to make sense of any talk about integrating Christian beliefs with mathematical equations. So I don't think anyone has ever suggested that when you are studying psychophysics, you should, as a Christian, add another constant into Weber's Law or to the Fechner fraction, on the grounds of Christian belief. If they did, they would be laughed out of court immediately.

I imagine we agree that being a Christian involves a commitment to truth. That can mean a lot of different things, I realize, but I suggest it at least means telling the story about anything as it really is, and, if there is a possible evidential basis for any statements you're making, then you should be able to point to these unambiguously. With this in mind, one author wrote, I think helpfully, "Without [adherence to the scientific standards of 'show me'], professional psychology and psychotherapy become a matter of 'views' and 'schools,' with the result that they are highly influenced by cultural beliefs and fads."[2]

Another author, writing at the same time, reminds us, "Reality is the overseer at one's shoulder, ready to rap one's knuckles or to spring the trap into which one has been led by overconfidence, or by a too-complacent reliance on mere surmise. Science succeeds precisely because it has accepted a bargain in which even the boldest imagination stands hostage to reality.

Reality is the unrelenting angel with whom scientists have agreed to wrestle."[3] In the context of what we are talking about, the magnitude of the problem becomes apparent when you realize that within the psychological marketplace today, it is estimated that there are more than 250 varieties of psychotherapy on offer. The role of nonpsychological influences into psychotherapy was well illustrated a decade or so ago by the intrusion of beliefs from the New Age movement.

Malcolm,

Thank you for that recommended reading and for your comments. My question now is if your view of the mind-brain relationship and the psychobiological unity of humans raises issues for the psychotherapist or counselor, whichever of the 250 schools they may belong to?

Ben,

You have reminded me that, historically, within the Christian tradition, part of the pastoral task, formerly performed by clergy and pastors, was what used to be called "soul care." There is no doubt that some clergy were, and still are, wise counselors and, though they did not use this term, they gave much appreciated psychotherapy.

"Soul talk" continues to be heard loud and clear when evangelistic crusades are taking place, focusing on "saving souls." Coming to terms with the widely held view among evangelical biblical scholars—that any view of the soul as a "separate thing" is hard to justify from Scripture—means that we are in a difficult transition period in how we use "soul talk." Certainly the Christian idea of what I would call "soulishness" has a long and revered tradition and has served us well. I see no reason why it should not be retained if the concept of soul is understood as a brain-emergent human capacity with which we are able to experience personal relationships. This helps us to remember that persons develop and evolve in the context of relatedness with our fellow humans and, if we are Christians, with God.

Malcolm,

Yes, but how does that apply to what a psychotherapist or counseling psychologist actually does?

Ben,

I suppose what you are asking is, in the context of things like psychotherapy and counseling, does it really matter whether we think we have a thing called the soul or not? In short, does the view we hold about ourselves and about the nature of persons have any wider implications for things like counseling and psychotherapy?

One Christian writer on this topic, Virginia Todd Holeman, has suggested that "the view of personhood that takes the tightening in mind brain links seriously leads to a particular understanding of the metapurpose of Christian counseling with specific attention to the role of the Holy Spirit in general and the counseling relationship in particular."[4] In support of her views, she refers to evidence from a study by Lambert and others showing that there are four common factors that contribute to therapeutic success, regardless of the theoretical orientation of the therapist. Lambert notes, for example, that the rate of spontaneous recovery is about 40 percent, while use of a particular therapeutic technique ranked far down the list of things that bring about a change, estimated at about 15 percent. So Holeman raises the question, "If techniques matter so little in comparison with client factors, might it not suggest that specifically 'Christian techniques,' while they would be nice, are not absolutely necessary for Christian counseling to occur?" She argues, "It is not the external strategies that define Christian counseling, but the agency of the kingdom of God in the lives of counselors who seek to bring this healing reality to bear upon the lives of clients. The person of the therapist-in-relation-to-God brings the Christian into Christian counseling. In effect Christian counseling is less about technique and more about relationality."[5]

There is a lot to mull over there. If you want to follow this up I can point you to the writings of Christian psychotherapists and counselors like Virginia Holeman who take seriously the evidence from neuropsychology pointing to the unity of the human person. Such evidence underlining our psychobiological unity has increased rapidly with the advent of techniques like MRI. Its increasing use already holds out hope of shedding new light on old problems. For example, in 2011 a report was published of structural neuroimaging studies in major depressive disorders.[6] The investigators carried out a meta-analysis of 143 MRI studies that had measured the brain structures of people with depression. They compared these findings with those from research with bipolar disorder. They found that people with clinical depression showed reductions in the grey matter of the brain, including reduced volume of the frontal lobe, basal ganglia and hippocampus. Bipolar disorder, by contrast, was associated with reductions in white matter. Such research points to the next steps, such as discovering when and how the brain changes occur. And if it is possible to answer that, then ultimately it should be possible to treat depression more effectively. We must be suspicious, however, of claims to have found how to treat all forms of depression, whether by psychotherapy or psychopharmacology.

16

Are Religious Beliefs the Twenty-First-Century Opium of the People?

What About Placebo Effects?

Malcolm,

Do you believe that religious beliefs are what you have called "top-down" effects? If so, does that explain the claimed health benefits of religious beliefs and maybe even the placebo effects of religious beliefs?

The topic of placebo effects came up in class when our lecturer said that work at the interface of psychology and neuroscience was providing a scientific basis for how beliefs (which he said were examples of "top down" effects) could influence health and behavior. I think he was hinting, but not actually saying, that the placebo effect could help explain things like prayer as being a sort of self-induced helpline, and how religious beliefs could improve general health and quality of life for some people. Can you help me on this?

Ben,

I wonder if your lecturer had just read the *Times*? Only the other day it reported a meeting of the British Medical Association at which a vote was taken agreeing that homeopathic medicines should no longer be provided by the National Health Service. The report said that one of the participants had argued that if a patient wanted to have one of these medicines, it should be labeled as a placebo. So your question, while topical, is part of a long, ongoing and wider debate.

Its true that these and similar seemingly throwaway remarks of your lecturer, speculating on the placebo effect, are at times used to try and explain why there is evidence that religion is linked with better health. It goes back more than a century when religion was described as "the opium of the masses." Perhaps your lecturer was implying that what we now know about the placebo effect shows that was true after all. Claiming, in effect, that now we know how the "opium" works through the placebo effect of religious belief. That would fit with the extensive evidence that, on average, better health is enjoyed by those who are religious—something that seems to have been missed by some of today's "new atheists" who argue that faith is toxic! Your lecturer could also be hinting at yet another way of explaining away religion.

Malcolm,

Can you tell me more about this? If religious belief is nothing more than a kind of placebo effect, and that causes the reported better health among religious people, what does this do to our understanding that there's something special about religious belief, about being grounded in a relationship with a God who really exists?

Ben,

For details of the evidence for the links between religious belief and health, have a look at David Myers's textbook.[1] He summarizes the present state of play, from the evidence currently available, of the possible placebo effects of religious beliefs and religious practices.

A central question is how a belief, whether it is true or not, can produce a therapeutic effect. A century of work in neuroscience has shown how our subjective experience of ourselves and the world around us depends on the precise workings of billions of nerve cells, and probably also on trillions of ever-changing connections between these cells. It is clear that changes in our subjective sensations, feelings and ideas are fundamentally tied to corresponding alterations in neural activity. We may not yet fully understand the nature of the relationship between subjective mental phenomena (mind) and observable brain processes (body), but advances in neuroscience have established an intimate link between the two.

Recognizing this link opens up new possibilities of correlating mental phenomena such as belief or faith with a range of effects in the physical body. The question remains, how does this link develop and how does it work? From the standpoint of neuroscience, beliefs are complex cognitive patterns that have both genetic and environmental causes. So, to the extent that the neural underpinnings of belief can, for example, be plausibly linked to the neural antecedents of healing, a biological connection between faith and healing becomes a scientifically testable issue. In the case of the placebo effect this is sometimes used to demonstrate, for example, how beliefs may help to relieve pain.

A typical study of the placebo effect in relieving pain would train people with an infusion of morphine and then show how a subsequent infusion of an inert solution (salt water), which the participant believes is morphine, can dramatically reduce their reported pain. People vary in showing the placebo effect. Brain imaging in subjects who show a robust placebo analgesia confirms their subjective reports by showing reduced activity in the brain areas normally activated by painful stimuli. In addition, other brain areas, including those activated by the powerful painkiller morphine, show increased activity. Finally, the analgesic effect of placebo can be reversed by a molecule that blocks the brain's receptors for opioids. So it seems that the degree of expectation for recovery that religious belief or faith potentially exerts, produces its greatest healing effect by fostering confidence that there will be a positive outcome. So insofar as there is any evidence, it points to a real and measurable effect of beliefs on bodily processes such as felt pain. It doesn't explain pain away, and it doesn't explain beliefs away.

Malcolm,

I found that fascinating! Now I'm curious to know more about how brain imaging has been used to study the placebo effect.

Ben,

I wasn't sure how interested you were in this, so I limited myself to beliefs and placebo effects. To answer your question about how using the rapid developments in sophisticated brain imaging techniques might be used to investigate how the placebo effect might work, let me give you an example.

Mario Beauregard mobilized the resources of the departments of radiology, psychology, neuropsychology and neurology at his university. He claims, "The results of the neuroimaging studies of placebo confirm that the patient's beliefs and expectations play a pivotal role in [the placebo] effect. These results also corroborate the notion that the placebo effect can be extremely specific." He goes on, "Taken together, the results of the neuroimaging studies of placebo effect demonstrate that beliefs and expectations can markedly modulate neurophysiological and neurochemical activity in brain regions involved in perception, movement, pain, and various aspects of emotion processing."[2]

The moment you try to harness the power of the placebo effect, you run up against serious ethical issues. Should doctors, for example, take the morally dubious step of tricking their patients into thinking a prescribed pill has an active ingredient when, in fact, it does not? A recent study by Professor Ted Kaptchuk at Harvard Medical School suggests that when dealing with patients with irritable bowel syndrome (IBS), even when they were told that the pills they were given had no active ingredient but were also told that "placebo pills, something like sugar pills, have been shown in rigorous clinical testing to produce significant mind-body self-healing processes," they still reported improved symptom relief relative to a control group. The researchers comment, "Our results suggest that the placebo response is not necessarily neutralized when placebos are administered openly."[3] Fascinating. However, the sample size of the study was small—37 experimental, 43 control—so the jury remains out on whether the actual use of placebos remains consistent with evidence-based medicine.

Recently researchers used fresh techniques for obtaining MRI images of the spinal cord, something that, in the past, has been difficult because of its small size and its being surrounded by airways and pulsating arteries. Now, however, these researchers, using advances in image processing, obtained high-resolution scans of the region. They studied the spinal cords of fifteen healthy volunteers using functional magnetic resonance imaging, and they focused in on an area called the dorsal horn, which transmits pain signals coming up through the spinal cord into the pain-related areas in the brain. During the scan, the volunteers received laser pinpricks to their hands. They were told that pain relief cream had been applied to one of their hands and control cream to the other. Unknown to the volunteers, an identical control cream was administered to both hands. When the participants believed they had received the active cream, they "reported feeling 25% less pain and showed significantly reduced activity in the spinal cord pathway that processes pain." Previously it had been shown the placebo causes the release of natural opioids in areas of the brain involved in pain control, such as the rostral anterior cingulate cortex. It was not known, however, whether natural opioids acted on the spinal cord in the same way as artificial painkillers or whether they simply changed people's tolerance or interpretation of pain. The researchers claimed, "We've shown that psychological factors can influence pain at the earliest stage of the central nervous system, in a similar way to drugs like morphine."[4]

But do be careful not to try and overgeneralize these findings. About one person in seven in the U.K. suffers from chronic pain or long-lasting pain of some kind, the most common being arthritis, back pain and headaches. But chronic pain comes in two main varieties. Inflammatory pain occurs when a persistent injury following a burn or in arthritis, for example, leads to an enhanced sensitivity of pain-sensitive nerve endings, leading to increased sensation of pain. But there is a more intractable variety of chronic pain, neuropathic pain, in which nerve damage causes ongoing pain and a hypersensitivity to stimuli.

The exciting news is that a group at Cambridge has identified a gene, called HCN2, responsible for regulating chronic pain. Neuropathic pain, often lifelong, is surprisingly common and difficult to treat with current drugs. These recent developments led by Professor Peter McNaughton, however, hold out new hope. He recently said, "Individuals suffering from neuropathic pain often have little or no respite because of the lack of effective medication. Our research lays the groundwork for the development of new drugs to treat chronic pain by blocking the HCN2."[5] I suspect that this type of chronic pain would be unlikely to show placebo effects.

Malcolm,

Thanks for those details. Do demonstrated effects of beliefs, including belief that our prayers have an effect, serve as evidence that our beliefs are true and that therefore God must exist?

Ben,

It's one thing to demonstrate, in some instances, the beneficial nature of religious faith, but whether or not that, in any sense, constitutes a proof of the existence of God is another matter. You cannot move from descriptions of what is the case, scientifically, to claiming it as support for metaphysical explanations. The extent to which faith healing, for example, is explainable by natural processes does not, of itself, constitute an argument for metaphysical or divine agency; unless, of course, you broaden your notion of what qualifies as "divine."

This topic of the effect of the mind on the body has a long history, and it is clear that today it is an area of research being actively pursued with fresh discoveries appearing every day. One thing is clear, however: there is a great danger in public pronouncements, of oversimplifying an extremely complex research topic, perhaps motivated by a wish for dramatic media headlines. As Christians we should have no part in this. I think it's also clear that there is the constant temptation, perhaps especially for those not closely involved in the field, to feel threatened by such research either when it is presented as "explaining away" their religious beliefs or, equally mistakenly, when it is used by some to seek to bolster religious belief by putting it forward as some sort of proof that there must be a God who is acting through these beliefs. I do hope we can heed these warnings.

17

What About Spirituality?

Is It a Separate "Religious" Part of Me?

Malcolm,

Obviously I have a lot to learn if I do qualify for further training in clinical psychology and psychotherapy. For now, at least, I think I am beginning to see a picture that does justice *both* to the possible therapeutic "top-down" effects of psychotherapy, such as those in cognitive behavior therapy, *and* to the need to give serious attention to "bottom-up" effects, such as ways in which changes in our brains, through accident or disease, can sometimes severely limit what can be achieved through psychotherapy alone. But what about what is often loosely referred to as a person's "spirituality"?

Can both "top-down" and "bottom-up" effects affect a person's spirituality?

I'd be grateful for some help on this if you've got the time. It's a personal issue for me and my family because my grandmother has developed Alzheimer's. She is, as you know, a lovely Christian woman and we have always thought of her as a deeply spiritual person. She gets very distressed because she has so much trouble praying and reading her Bible. What is happening to her ability to experience and enjoy spiritual activities?

Ben,

I'm so sorry to hear about your grandmother. It is unlikely that you will get much in your undergraduate lectures on Alzheimer's dementia, so I will say a bit about it in the hopes that it may bring you and your family some comfort as you watch your grandmother with her struggles and try to help in whatever way you can.

For a long time it's been recognized that the disease processes in cases of Alzheimer's show themselves in characteristic changes in the nerve cells in the brain. One change is the appearance of what are called neurofibrillary tangles, forming inside neurons. These tangles are remnants of microscopic tubes that normally transport materials important to the cell's function throughout the neurons. In addition to these changes there are globules of what is called amyloid protein, which are deposited at the tips of neuron branches. These so-called senile plaques contain fragments of degenerating nerve cells. Some researchers think it's these deposits that are the root cause of the destruction of the nerve cells, but the debate is a very lively one.

It is now widely accepted that the clinical and neuropathological features of Alzheimer's disease arise *both* from environmental *and* genetic factors. At least five different genes have been identified as causing Alzheimer's disease. Biochemical analysis of the effects of mutations and polymorphisms in these genes has shown that they all affect the processing of the amyloid precursor protein and cause a buildup of a toxic fragment of this protein, called amyloid beta peptide. Identifying this unifying biochemical feature of the disease has already led to attempts to develop therapies that will block the accumulation of this neurotoxic amyloid beta peptide, and some of the therapies are already in human clinical trials.

Most recently, exciting research reported by Professor Barbara Sahakian at Cambridge University has shown how a simple test should make it possible to detect the onset of Alzheimer's disease much earlier. And early identification would, in turn, enable earlier intervention before damage is done. Professor Sahakian has devised a simple computerized cognitive task that can be used to detect mild cognitive impairment, which is very much the precursor stage to Alzheimer's.[1] The good news is that there are currently a number of neuroprotective drugs in development with the pharmaceutical industry for the treatment of Alzheimer's disease. Early detection combined with these new drugs when available holds out hope for the future.

From a psychological point of view, there is already a recognized list of features of Alzheimer's disease. Just to list them shows how distressing they can be. They include forgetfulness, agitation and aggression, depression, incontinence, suspicion, paranoia and psychotic behavior, wandering, language difficulties, apraxia and sleeping difficulties. When these distressing changes get translated into effects on a person's religious life or spirituality, they appear as loss of memory of one's formative spiritual experiences (of one's baptism, for example), an unreal fear of spiritually sinister forces with a sense of spiritual emptiness, a diminished participation in spiritual practices such as taking part in worship or reading the Scriptures and praying, difficulty in experiencing God's presence and comfort, an unreal experience of guilt about the loss of a close relationship with others in the community of faith and finally, an inability to carry out the acts of service to others that one has been used to doing. Altogether a devastating experience for a committed and devout Christian.

Just how devastating is underlined if you see how some of these effects map onto the six central aspects of Christian spirituality listed recently by Tom Wright.[2] Remembering that loss of memory is a prominent feature of Alzheimer's disease, you can see how devastating it is to be unable to remember some of your formative spiritual experiences such as new birth and baptism, first in Wright's list. Two more of the marks of spirituality, prayer and the reading of Scripture, are likewise affected. The capacity to give and respond to love, next in Wright's list, is radically altered in Alzheimer's patients. The final mark of spirituality is the Lord's Supper or Eucharist, and it's interesting that researchers like Glenn Weaver note how the simple act of breaking the bread and taking the wine brings renewed awareness of God's presence in Alzheimer's patients who otherwise are in a state of despair.[3]

Malcolm,

That was a great help. I shared it with my family and they asked me to say thank you.

Remembering the very tight link between mental processes and brain processes, and remembering the distressing changes in spirituality in Alzheimer's, does that mean that the spiritual part of life is embodied in our physical makeup?

Ben,

Today, *spirituality* has become a buzzword. It seems to be used to refer to everything from the activities of monks when praying, to New Age experiences, forms of magic, the use of Ouija boards and the use of drugs producing out-of-body experiences. For some people spirituality is a sort of controlled religious high, often devoid of almost all the precise content that it would entail if one were talking about the spirituality of you and most of your church friends. You could reasonably ask, Would the same neural events be considered religious or spiritual if someone had no religious background whatsoever? Of course, you could reply, as some do, that spirituality is all to do with the soul and that the soul is not physical or material. But, if that is so, why is your grandmother's spirituality so challenged by her Alzheimer's disease?

Cambridge psychologist and theologian Fraser Watts has helpfully suggested that we should distinguish three different uses of the term *spiritual healing*: first is "healing in which spiritual practices play a role"; second is "healing in which spiritual aspects of the human person are presumed to be involved"; third is healing "explained in terms of what are presumed to be spiritual processes."[4] I believe that Watts's further suggestion, if kept in mind, helps to avoid confusing and mixing up categories. He writes, "The key question is not whether spiritual healing is to be understood scientifically *or* theologically, but what the relationship should be between theological and scientific accounts."[5] And you will know that we have discussed this before and I have reminded you that in studying any piece of human behavior or experience, you may give an *exhaustive* account at one level, the psychobiological, but that without further warrant you may not claim that this is the *exclusive* and only account relevant to a full understanding of all that is being studied.

Malcolm,

From what you say, it sounds like everyone with Alzheimer's finds it affecting their spirituality. But some of my friends have relatives with Alzheimer's who still participate in some church activities. Does that not point to a separate, immaterial soul unaffected by the Alzheimer's changes to the brain?

Ben,

I see your point. We have to be rather careful we don't overstate the case, as if we now fully understand the link between changes in the brain during Alzheimer's disease and a person's spirituality. A good counter to jumping to such a conclusion is a study of a group of nuns. The participants were 678 American members of the School Sisters of Notre Dame religious congregation who were aged 75-106. An earlier report described one of the participants, Sister Mary, as "the gold standard for the Nun study." Sister Mary was a remarkable woman who had high cognitive test scores before her death at 101 years of age. Incredibly, she maintained this high status despite having abundant evidence of the presence of the classical lesions of Alzheimer's disease in her brain—namely, neurofibrillary tangles and senile plaques. The findings from Sister Mary and the other participants in the nun study undoubtedly produce fresh clues about the etiology of aging in Alzheimer's disease as it develops. They also suggest how the clinical expression of some diseases may be averted.[6]

One may ask, as you do, does not the evidence from Sister Mary undermine the notion of the strong relationship between brain and mind we have already talked about? I think the answer is no. What it does do is make us think much harder about the nature of these relationships and recognize how much more we have to learn. We have to ask why Sister Mary's experiences were different from those of, for example, a Christian in a different ecclesiastical tradition. I have in mind the high-profile Presbyterian Minister Robert Davis.

Robert Davis was diagnosed with Alzheimer's dementia when he was fifty-three and at the height of his ministerial career. With the help of his wife, he wrote a remarkable account of his spiritual experiences well into the middle stages of the disease. It documents how his progressive brain disease affected his spirituality. It is graphically illustrated in his own words. He wrote,

> My spiritual life was still most miserable. I could not read the Bible. I could not pray as I wanted because my emotions were dead and cut off. There was no feedback from God the Holy Spirit. . . . My mind could not rest and grow calm but instead raced relentlessly, thinking dreadful thoughts of despair.
>
> My mind also raced about, grasping for the comfort of the Savior whom I knew and loved and for the emotional peace that he could give me, but

> finding nothing. I concluded that the only reason for such darkness must be spiritual. Unnamed guilt filled me. Yet the only guilt I could put a name to was failure to read my Bible. But I could not read, and would God condemn me for this? I could only lie there and cry, "Oh God, why? Why?" [7]

Davis says further, "I can no longer be spiritually fed by sermons. I can get the first point of the sermon and then I am lost. The rest of it sends my mind whirling in a jumble of twisted unconnected ideas. . . . Coughing, headache, and great discomfort have attended my attempts to be fed in all the ways I am accustomed to meeting God through his Word."[8]

It is heartrending to read this. You will have noticed that Robert's was an instance of early-onset Alzheimer's. Sister Mary's may have been late-onset, and therein may lie part of the reason for the different effects in the two cases since we do not yet understand the detailed neurological differences between early- and late-onset Alzheimer's.

Malcolm,

Are there other diseases that affect spirituality?

Ben,

Yes, indeed there are. Another very distressing illness, suffered alike by Christians and non-Christians, is depression. Just to mention depression should set warning lights flashing. You have to be careful when talking about depression as if it is just one illness. Any psychiatrist will tell you that it presents itself in a variety of ways and almost certainly with a variety of etiologies. How one seeks to help a depressed person depends very much on whether, to oversimplify, the person is mildly depressed or is suffering from a moderate or severe depressive illness.

At times you may come across the triumphalist way that I have heard some people present the Christian faith, which implies that if you suffer from depression you must have fallen away from the faith or committed some undisclosed sin. That approach, mercifully, is much less common today than it once was. Partly to counter such gross distortions of the truth, a prominent Christian, Lewis Smedes, a former professor at Fuller Theological Seminary, wrote about his experiences of depression in his book *My God and I.* He noted his feelings of helplessness and alienation from God during that time.[9]

Smedes describes the alleviation of his depression in this way: "Then God came back. He broke through my terror and said: 'I will never let you fall. I will always hold you up.'. . . I felt as if I had been lifted from a black pit straight up into joy." Smedes adds the following comment, "I have not been neurotically depressed since that day, though I must, to be honest, tell you that God also comes to me each morning and offers me a 20-milligram capsule of Prozac. . . . I swallow every capsule with gratitude to God."[10]

Malcolm,

What are your thoughts about how we, as Christians, should approach those with Alzheimer's?

Ben,

You and I both realize that our fellow Christians are constantly challenged, not only by the distressing effects of things like Alzheimer's disease and depression, but also by the everyday challenges to our lives as Christians. I think it's extremely important to remember that it is possible to get so preoccupied with studying the psychological, neurological, biochemical and physiological mechanisms underlying some of these distressing conditions that we find ourselves adopting a predominantly spectator account to the predicament of our fellow Christians. The true compassion to which all of us as Christians are called prompts us to do our best to empathize with our friends' suffering and to give them all the support we can.

In trying to take a balanced view on this, I think we need to recognize, as I've pointed out, that there are changes in our brains that may occur through no choices of our own. Alzheimer's disease was typically thought to be a classic case of this. And yet only this morning I was hearing of a very recent piece of research indicating that for at least some of the people who develop Alzheimer's disease, and the research suggested as much as a fifth, the disease could be significantly delayed or averted altogether through changes in lifestyle in midlife. So it's not inevitable.

The cumulative effect of knowledge of environmental and social factors on disease has the potential to make us more responsible for our actions, and at the same time more compassionate and attentive to the plight of those who, through no fault of their own, suffer diseases of the mind. It's so easy to blame the environment for our failures while being very quick to take credit for our successes. I think this means that our attitude toward others should be to take very seriously the research I've mentioned showing how people may be significantly influenced by their biology and their social, environmental and cultural contexts.

I think this also alerts us to the possibility that there will be changes in our spiritual awareness and consciousness of the presence and power of God, which are not immune to changes in our bodies in general and in our brains in particular. Going back to what I'm sure you will regard as one of my themes, the Bible's teaching about our psychobiological unity, none of this should come as a surprise. In taking a balanced view of this new knowledge about the relation between the brain and spirituality, we need to be vigilant. I think the "reductionist trap" is all too often set in our path. To fall into it would be rather like claiming that, for example, by analyzing the composition and distribution of the paints in an artist's masterpiece we have thereby shown that it is, after all, "nothing but" paint on canvas. If only we will stand back and look at the whole and get the picture into perspective, we shall be able to appreciate the masterpiece for what it is. To study man's mind and brain scientifically, including spirituality, does not necessarily threaten the dignity of man. Properly used, such knowledge can enable us to treat one another with greater dignity and understanding.

For those like you who have the privilege to study neuroscience and psychology to an advanced level, there is the opportunity to express your Christian compassion by getting into serious research of, for example, the deeper understanding of the neuronal changes occurring in Alzheimer's disease.

Such scientific research is demanding. It can involve long days and sometimes long nights in the laboratory, but it has the potential of enormous payoff in terms of the relief of human suffering. I know I'm going off on a tangent a bit here, but it does worry me when I hear preachers talk about going into "full-time Christian work." If we are Christians we should all be full-time Christians. And a dedicated career in research in neuroscience is no more and no less Christian than one as a pastor. Indeed, when we remember our Lord's deep concern to relieve suffering and show compassion, you would be truly following in his footsteps and obeying his commands if, through your research into Alzheimer's, the suffering of millions would be reduced or avoided. There will be no quick solutions here.

Today I read of a disappointing outcome of a study involving ten thousand people with Alzheimer's disease who had been using a new drug to tackle the buildup of a plaque called beta amyloid in their brains. Sadly the drug was not doing what it was designed to do. But that is not the end of the story. For the research will go on in attacking the underlying neurological problems in Alzheimer's disease, and you could be part of that effort. What could be more Christian than that? Compare such long-term, widespread effects with the so-called healing campaigns that occasionally take place at local churches, where perhaps a handful of people claim to get short-term remission from some of their symptoms only to be back where they were again in a few months, and you will see why a dedicated research career has the potential to relieve the sufferings of countless people.

Malcolm,

I just remembered something I meant to ask you when I had a course of lectures on individual differences. The lecturer talked about how some of us are more introverted, some more extroverted, some more neurotic and so on. As we looked at some of the questionnaires used to measure these things, I began to wonder what this might imply about becoming and being a Christian?

According to the lecturer, some of these cognitive and personality characteristics appear to have a biological basis. So since we're all different in our abilities to think logically, trust others and so on, does this mean that it's more difficult for some people to become Christians than others?

Ben,

You have raised some very important and profound issues. Let me try and point you to how I think about this. When the apostle Paul is trying to help the young Christians at Ephesus, he talks about how their faith began and how it continues. Look at Ephesians 2:8-10, which I'll quote in Tom Wright's own translation. Paul wrote, "You have been saved by grace, through faith. This doesn't happen on your own initiative; it is God's gift. It isn't on the basis of works and no one is able to boast. This is the explanation: God has made us what we are. God has created us in King Jesus for the good works that he prepared, ahead of time, as the road we must travel." Later commenting on it, Wright says, "Faith is not something that humans do to make themselves acceptable to God. Nothing we can do, unaided, can achieve that. If there were such a thing, it would become a matter of our initiative, and *the people who had this ability* would be able to hold their heads up in pride over those who didn't. On the contrary. Because it's all a matter of God's gift, there is no room for any human being to boast."[11] Those words I have put in italics give a clue to answer your questions about whether this or that "ability" enables people to become Christians.

This reminds us why becoming a Christian is all, and entirely, because of God's initiative and his love for us, and this passage in Ephesians is all about the grace of God. It's not something that God gives me to help me out of a tight corner here or there when normally I can get on fine without him. It's not something just to enhance my ordinary life. Rather, grace is about the fact that God's love gives life to the dead. It is God's free, undeserved gift. According to Paul, our salvation is God's responsibility. It comes about through grace. Working out our salvation is a long, demanding process. Paul has no doubts about that, and our individual differences express themselves in the glorious diversity of fulfilled Christian lives that we are privileged to see in any lively, loving, Christian community.

18

Can Science "Explain Away" Religion?

Malcolm,

Your emails have pointed out that the same evidence is often interpreted in very different ways. For example, some Christians point to the evidence that certain parts of the brain are active during prayer, and they try to use that as proof for the existence of God. Others understand the same evidence as showing that praying to God is "nothing but" the selective activity of specific brain areas. Can you help me understand how to properly relate scientific findings to Christian beliefs?

Ben,

The question you raise has cropped up repeatedly as we have discussed how to relate scientific accounts of human life to other accounts, including the religious. There is undoubtedly an ever-present temptation, to which some have succumbed, to believe that scientific descriptions can reduce human life, including religion, to nothing more than biological, physical or psychological processes.

An unthinking commitment to reductionism crops up even in the writings of our most illustrious scientists. For example, Francis Crick, whom I've mentioned before, wrote in his book *The Astonishing Hypothesis,* "You are no more than the behavior of a vast assembly of nerve cells and their associated molecules. . . . You are nothing but a pack of neurons."[1] I mentioned earlier in our correspondence that the logical conclusion to Crick's approach would be that his own written words are "nothing but" ink strokes on the page carrying their message. But even he drew back from that at the end of the book when he wrote, "The words 'nothing but' in our hypothesis can be misleading if understood in too naive a way." Crick's fellow Nobel laureate Roger Sperry alerted to the dangers of reductionism when he wrote, "The meaning of the message will not be found in the chemistry of the ink."[2]

Only recently I came across another instance of this when a respected and high-profile neuroscientist in Britain, Professor Colin Blakemore, was talking about "God and the Scientist" when taking part in the Channel 4 series titled *Christianity and History.* Among other things, he expressed the hope that "science will one day explain everything including the human need for religious belief." He probably had in mind the suggestion that has been made that we have developed brains with properties that inevitably produce a predisposition to belief in a God or in gods. This then means (so he implies) that our beliefs in God are "nothing but" the selective chattering of the neurons of our brain.

The problem with this sort of argument, which Colin Blakemore failed to point out, is that it applies equally to his views about the possibility that one day science will explain everything including the human need for religious belief. In terms of his argument, his views are "nothing but" the chattering of the neurons in *his* brain. In effect, this kind of appeal to reductionism really gets you nowhere and never takes seriously the arguments being put forward about why people believe or do not believe. The point is that these have to be taken seriously on their own merits. The same applies to properly interpreting the results from studies of the genetics or social psychology of religion and religious behavior. These are simultaneously a study of irreligiosity since they frequently compare more and less religious people. Hence Colin Blakemore's irreligiosity is put under the microscope, but that does not explain away any grounds for his irreligiosity that he puts forward. These must be considered on their own merits.

Malcolm,

I shared with some of my Christian friends what you said about explaining and explaining away. Some said that even long before the challenges from neuroscience, Freud had already explained religion away using psychology, claiming it was all wishful thinking. What do you say about that?

Ben,

Your friends were right. There have been many attempts to explain the origin of religion, whether by anthropologists or psychologists or, as we were saying, more recently from neuroscientists such as Colin Blakemore. Broadly speaking, when psychologists have taken an interest in religion they have concentrated on what we might call its roots and its fruits—questions about the origins of religion and questions about how religious people should behave.

Since your friends raised it, here is a bit of detail. In the twentieth century Sigmund Freud's radical views became widely known, and the stage was set for a strong resurgence of what has been called the "warfare metaphor" when discussing how science and religion are related. According to Freud the practices of religions are "nothing but" the persistence of what, using his psychoanalytic terminology, is an "interim social neurosis." He said that we must eventually grow out of this.

Freud wrote at length about this in *The Future of an Illusion* and *Civilization and Its Discontents*.[3] According to Freud, an "illusion" stands for any belief system based on human wishes. He was careful to point out that such a basis does not necessarily imply that the system is false; nevertheless, as far as Christianity was concerned, he clearly believed that it was. In that sense he was championing and perpetuating the warfare metaphor.

A major problem for the psychoanalytic treatment of religion as being the product of unconscious wishes, or for any effort to explain religion away, is that such an explanation can be applied equally well to the understanding of unbelief. This was penetratingly demonstrated by Rumke in his little book *The Psychology of Unbelief*.[4] In it he looked carefully at the history of Freud's own life—such as his poor relationships with his father and his intense dislike of his Roman Catholic nanny—and he put these together to show how, on the basis of Freud's own theory, a picture emerges from which we would predict that a person with such a background would, on reaching maturity, produce a rationalized set of beliefs in which he would reject religion, particularly a religion in which God was seen as a father figure. And Freud did just that. Likewise today's atheist skeptics reflect certain cultural influences—they manifest the thinking styles of western white males (which they are).

Malcolm,

Your comments were helpful. I had just been talking with some friends about the nature of faith, and someone said they heard that psychologists had shown it to be "wishful thinking." We also got to talking about doubt. One of the group said that doubt is the opposite of faith, and that doubt shows a lack of faith. Someone else suggested that doubt is sinful. What do you think about that?

Ben,

Your question takes us back to psychology fifty years ago. The leading personality theorist at that time was Professor Gordon Allport at Harvard. He was a Christian and wrote a book titled *The Individual and His Religion: A Psychological Interpretation.* I mention it now because he had a chapter titled "The Nature of Doubt." Allport argued that constructive doubt could lead to greater faith.[5]

Mention of Gordon Allport's book, with its penetrating psychological analysis of the nature of doubt, brings to mind the part played by constructive doubt in the life of Robert Boyle, an early fellow of the Royal Society in Britain. Reijer Hooykaas, in a chapter titled "Boyle's Life and Times," records how after his "conversion," Boyle, according to a fragment of an autobiography, "made a vow to repent, and respond to Christ, 'who had long lain asleep in his conscience.'" This was followed, Hooykaas tells us, "by grave doubts about some of the fundamentals of Christianity." These doubts were followed by depression and "only the fact that the Christian religion forbade it kept him from taking his own life." However, Hooykaas also records, "One day after receiving the sacrament, God restored to him the lost sense of his favor." Thereafter he was from time to time subject to what he called a "disease of my faith," but, writes Hooykaas, "it brought him to the grounds of his religion, for doubt impelled him to give an account of the fundamentals of Christianity."[6] Hooykaas notes how Boyle declared that "He whose Faith never Doubted, may justly doubt of his Faith."[7]

Honest questioning is a biblical route to deeper faith. Athol Dickson has reminded us of this, referring to his own experience when he wrote, "At the church of my youth, I somehow got the idea that only a prideful person would dare to question the Lord. . . . I have learned that sometimes asking questions is a way to demonstrate humility, because inherent in the question is the assumption that I do not have the answer; God does. Sincere questions give God respect. They acknowledge his power. They honor him."[8]

In his book he reminds us how questioning God occurs throughout Scripture. Abraham asks questions of God. Look at Genesis 18. So does Moses. The take-home message from this, says Dickson, is that "asking is not doubting. It is trusting." He adds, "How wonderful now to know that I can question the Lord without fear of faithlessness!" And he later adds, "In my own life, fear of questioning God accomplished the reverse of Peter's admonition to 'always be prepared to give an answer to everyone who asks you to give the reason for the hope that you have.' Until I began to question God . . . I knew *what* I believed, but I had only a superficial idea *why* I believed. Paranoia masquerading as awe kept me ignorant of the deeper truths God has commanded me to explain."[9]

All of this resonates with Gordon Allport's statement that "if each person understood the doubting process, he would be in a better position to determine the cogency of his own grounds for belief or disbelief."[10] I think Allport was a good role model for all Christians when, reminding us of the superficiality of quick, slick solutions, he wrote, "Different as are science and art in their axioms and methods they have learned to cooperate in a thousand ways—in the production of fine dwellings, music, clothing, design. Why should not science and religion, likewise differing in axioms and method, yet cooperate in the production of an improved human character without which all other human gains are tragic loss? From many sides today comes the demand that religion and psychology busy themselves in finding a common ground for uniting their efforts for human welfare."[11]

Malcolm,

One of my lecturers has talked about some of the great psychologists of the last century, especially the behaviorist psychologist B. F. Skinner and neuropsychologist Roger Sperry. I wonder whether either of these had any views on religion? Did they try to explain religion away?

Ben,

Yes, Professor Skinner was indeed enormously influential in the last century, and he did try to explain religion away. Having developed techniques for shaping and modifying behavior, he speculated about whether such techniques could be harnessed to shape the future of society. Regarding religion, he speculated about whether some forms of religion were in fact based on a system of rewards and punishments, as were his behavior-shaping techniques. So he saw the ultimate punishment as hell and believed some religious groups used that threat very effectively. In Skinner's view, good things are personified in the notion of God and can be used to shape religious behavior either because they promise great benefits or, as he believed in the case of hell, because it was a very strong aversive stimulus. Anyway, he thought that some religious groups used both to try and shape the behavior of those who followed their views.

At the end of the day he was another example of those who try to reduce religion to "nothing but" some form of science. Roger Sperry took quite a different view. He was one of the founders of the cognitive revolution in psychology. He spoke and wrote about what he called the "bankruptcy" of some forms of behaviorism. In his view, religious beliefs are not necessarily in conflict with science but mutually compatible. But I have to tell you that some of Sperry's views on religion would sound very strange to any remotely orthodox Christian.

In Britain arguably the most influential psychologist of the second half of the last century was Sir Frederick Bartlett, professor of psychology at Cambridge. He was another of the architects of the cognitive revolution. According to his view, any final decision about the validity or value of any claims made by religious people had to be judged on the basis of the evidence. He said that being a psychologist gives him neither superior nor inferior authority in these matters.[12]

Malcolm,

That is helpful. While we're talking about how to relate what I'm learning in my science with my wider beliefs, including my Christian beliefs, can I ask a related question? A friend who is studying zoology told me about recent evidence that the need for religion is the natural outcome of evolutionary development. Am I right in understanding this as another attempt to explain religion away?

Ben,

Today there is a resurgence of interest in understanding the origins of religion and in attempting to understand why people have religious beliefs. Some of this comes from areas of science where psychology links up, for example, with evolutionary biology and neuroscience. I imagine this is what your friend studying zoology has heard about.

Justin Barrett, together with many collaborators worldwide, has been reporting crosscultural studies of how young children, up to the age of five, develop their views of the supernatural.[13] Barrett begins with the assumption, reasonably well grounded, that there is strong biological and cognitive continuity with ancestral species and nonhuman primates. He notes that there is a widely held belief that religious thoughts may be regarded as evolutionary byproducts.

Barrett suggests that his early research findings in the development of teleological reasoning point to one possible cognitive reason for the culturally widespread existence of religious beliefs in a variety of deities.

Another result from child development studies is to underline how "intuitive" religious thought is. But there are differences of opinion about how to interpret these findings. Barrett also believes that the cognitive science study of religion shows that religious practices are adaptive, and that this adaptiveness has encouraged their persistence (either through genetic selection, cultural selection, or gene-culture co-evolution dynamics). A pervasive theme of these sorts of accounts is that religion and religious ideas and practices somehow yield communities of people that are more cooperative or prosocial than they would be otherwise.

Barrett is aware that you can interpret research findings in different ways depending on your presuppositions. He notes that Richard Dawkins, for example, uses similar data to "explain away" any belief in God—religion, he says, can all be explained naturally. Barrett himself sees no reason to draw such conclusions. Rather, he says, "perhaps such evidence could even be used as part of an argument affirming a divinely implanted receptivity to the transcendent." Quizzed further about this research, Barrett adds, "This project does not set out to prove God or gods exist. Just because we find it easier to think in a particular way does not mean that it is true in fact. If we look at why religious beliefs and practices persist in societies across the world, we conclude that individuals bound by religious ties might be more likely to cooperate as societies."[14] The debate will continue. As you probably know, Justin Barrett is himself an active Christian, now a professor at Fuller Theological Seminary.

Linking evolutionary psychology with cognitive neuroscience to understand religion is also certainly in the news. In 2009 the *New Scientist* ran an article titled "Natural Born Believers," with the subheading "Why Religion Is Part of Human Nature." Brains, it said, are primed for it.[15] The following month the National Academy of Sciences in America published a paper with the title "Cognitive and Neural Foundations of Religious Belief."[16] At the end of November in the same year, a paper appeared in the journal *Science* with the title "On the Origin of Religion." This time the appeal was to the results of new research in archaeology and anthropology, combined with emerging evidence of using fMRI brain scanning techniques to study the brains of people entertaining religious thoughts.[17]

It is all fascinating material. Presumably, similar approaches could be taken to studying the origins of political beliefs, or ethical beliefs or moral beliefs or indeed of scientific beliefs. Imagine that someone discovered which parts of our brains are most active when we are undertaking scientific research. Would that mean that what we write in our scientific journals is untrue? Of course not. New insights into the neural, evolutionary, psychological or anthropological origins and underpinning of beliefs could never tell us whether beliefs are true or false. That can only be decided by studying what is claimed to be the evidential basis for the belief and then carefully evaluating it. But if we are to follow the recent advice of John Stott, in what became the last book he wrote (*The Radical Disciple*), what we need today is a new generation of what he calls "radical conservatives." He says we need to learn to be radical in thinking about some of the traditions handed down within our own cultures, and that includes some of the traditions within our particular church denominations. At the same time, he argues that we should remain conservative in relation to Scripture, meaning that we should take seriously what Scripture says on issues on which it properly speaks.[18] So, for us as Christians, it matters a great deal whether Jesus Christ lived, taught, died and rose again. It matters whether the history of the people of Israel is well documented. No amount of neurologizing or psychologizing can explain away well-documented historical events, though lively debates will continue as to how to interpret those events.

There is another research area that, I believe, is poised to take off and from which we may expect some new insights into how people represent the idea of God or gods to themselves. This is research that will probably be led by specialists in the field of social cognition. I expect it to reveal some fascinating differences, not only between individuals within one religious group, but also between different denominations and, on a wider canvas, between adherents of different religions. So watch this space. What none of this can do is be a substitute for answering the prior question of the evidential basis in history for any religious claims that are made. Either God exists or he does not, and no amount of psychologizing can conjure up a God who does not exist or get rid of a God who has revealed himself in history.

Malcolm,

So how do I relate my Christian beliefs to my neuroscientific and psychological knowledge?

Ben,

There have been many volumes written on that question. Christian philosopher Stephen Evans describes six ways in which Christians relate religious beliefs to psychological knowledge.[19] Perhaps the most widely accepted at the time of his writing was the view held by those who regard the different approaches to the same evidence as two different perspectives, the faith perspective and the science perspective. What Evans calls "perspectivalists" are, he says, those jealous to maintain the integrity of the scientific enterprise and to keep it unsullied by personal philosophies which at times are smuggled in unawares or undeclared. He believes that perspectivalism implies the incompleteness of science and this, he says, may be envisaged in two different ways. There are those who see the boundaries of science as territorial in nature. According to this view, he says, certain areas of reality are strictly off-limits to the scientific investigator. He labels such thinkers the "territorialist" kind. The other kind he portrays as those who see the scientific approach as only one of several possible ways of perceiving reality, hence the label "perspectivalist." Mary van Leeuwen, who has thought about these problems over many years, sees limitations in perspectivalism. She writes, "It seems to me that perspectivalism leaves too many unanswered questions to be the final word on the relationship between Christianity and psychology."[20]

I think the perspectivalist model has served us well and will, in many respects, continue to do so. Sometimes it has been portrayed as the plan and elevation drawings of a three-dimensional structure. Both contain important information, but any attempt to improperly intermix them will lead to confusion. They are not to be seen as competitors, but as necessary to provide a full picture of the reality they portray. This is essentially a static model of perspectivalism.

In thinking about this and trying to do full justice to the ongoing reciprocal interactions between science and faith, a more dynamic model would help. With this in mind, let me suggest how something you have learned in your psychology and neuroscience courses could turn out to be a helpful metaphor.

You will know that one of the most widely discussed current models of how the visual system works is that put forward by David Milner and Mel Goodale.[21] (I suppose I have a personal interest in this since both of them were members of the department in which I worked for so many years and were good colleagues, and I recruited both as young researchers and followed their glittering research careers with great pleasure.) Let me just remind you of their views.

As we look at the world around us, we pick up information through our senses of sight, smell, touch and taste. It is generally agreed that the visual system has to be able to accommodate two somewhat different functions—one concerned with acting on the world and the other with representing it. How the brain achieves these ends is intensively studied by neuropsychologists, neurophysiologists, neuroscientists and, more recently, computer scientists. The retina of the eye, as you know, which on embryological grounds can be considered part of the central nervous system, transduces the electromagnetic radiation hitting the photoreceptors into physiological signals that can be understood by the brain while at the same time performing several computations on those signals. From the retina there are numerous projections or pathways carrying different sorts of information to the so-called primary visual cortex and the higher visual areas of the cortex. Milner and Goodale claim, "Output requirements for a visual coding system serving the visual control of action are bound to be quite different from the requirements for a system subserving visual perception."[22] They note that "while it is true that different channels in the mammalian visual system are specialized for different kinds of visual analysis (broad band versus color opponent; magno versus parvo), at some point these separate inputs are combined and transformed in different ways for different purposes. In other words, both cortical streams process information about the intrinsic properties of objects and their spatial locations, but the transformations they carry out reflect the different purposes for which the two streams have evolved."[23] So they see what they call "a quasi-independence of the two visual streams," but they note that nevertheless "there will be reciprocal cross-connections between areas in the two streams."[24]

So, I asked, might this be a useful metaphor of how we may constructively relate and integrate the knowledge of ourselves and our world, through our science and our faith? As the visual system processes inputs, analyzes and uses them, and ultimately applies them for effective action, so we chart, analyze, process and integrate the knowledge of ourselves and our world, given, on the one hand, by the scientific enterprise, and on the other hand, in what God has chosen to reveal to us.

Thinking in this way helps remind us, first, that the data are not all of a kind, and to benefit fully, we must subject these data to appropriate forms of analysis. Both are important, both are relevant, but they are different. Second, after appropriate analysis in the relevant channel, information is brought together to enrich the total picture of the world that is available. Third, along the way there are opportunities for reciprocal cross-connections between the two streams that positively supplement and guide each other. Fourth, while the analysis from one stream is able to provide a detailed analysis of the world as it is, the analysis from the other stream is primarily given to make possible effective action in the world as it is.

Does this perhaps not remind us that, while through the scientific enterprise we gain a remarkable understanding of the way the world is, we also discover through what God reveals to us and teaches us in Scripture how to act within the world as we find it?

The two streams are not conflicting or competing; rather, they are complementary and enrich one another to the benefit of both. Is this not the way we should think about how positively and productively to integrate the knowledge given in the distinct domains of science and faith?

19

Where Next?

Malcolm,

As you survey the current scientific landscape, do you see significant developments on the horizon? Perhaps ones that may call for rethinking some of our long-held Christian beliefs?

Ben,

I'm sure you realize that anything I can say can only be one man's snapshot of a vast landscape of contemporary research. Things move so fast it's almost impossible to keep up. For what it's worth, here is my own take on where things seem to be moving.

The largest group of psychological scientists in the US are the members of the Association for Psychological Science. In 2009 they asked some of their lead researchers to give their personal views on where things seem to be moving at the beginning of the twenty-first century in the journal *Perspectives on Psychological Science*. It makes fascinating reading. You won't be surprised that I was encouraged when I saw that the first paper was titled "The Future of Psychology: Connecting Mind to Brain," by Lisa Feldman Barrett.[1] Since this has been the focus of much of our conversations, let me share with you some of her views.

The opening sentences of her abstract set the scene well: "Psychological states such as thoughts and feelings are real. Brain states are real. The problem is that the two are not real in the same way, creating the mind-brain correspondence problem." She adds, "Mind-brain, and relatedly, behavior-brain, correspondence continue to be the *central issues in psychology, and they remain the largest challenge in 21st-century psychology*."[2]

We've discussed how research on a common problem is frequently undertaken at several different levels. Barrett comments that "there must be an explicit accounting [that is, a mapping] of how categories at each level relate to one another."[3] She later writes, "The more important reason to avoid material reduction is that the various phenomena we are discussing [complex psychological categories, psychological primitives and neuronal firing] each exist at different levels of scientific inquiry and do not exist at others."[4]

I think she makes a very important point. If it is remembered, then the temptation to talk about psychological functions being reduced to the activity in your neurons will hopefully be avoided.

Another comment of Barrett's worth remembering is, "The complex psychological categories we refer to as thoughts, memories, emotions, and beliefs, or automatic processing, control processing, or the self, and so on, are observer dependent. They are collections of mental states that *are products of the brain, but they do not correspond to brain organisation in a one-to-one fashion*."[5]

Malcolm,

Yes, this affirms a theme of our conversation—that different levels of explanation each have their own integrity. And are there other areas of cognitive neuroscience that look set for fresh advances?

Ben,

Yes. I have just read a thought-provoking special section, "Mysteries of the Brain," in the journal *Science*. With the conference of the Society of Neuroscientists just ahead, where tens of thousands of neuroscientists gather annually, the editors of *Science* quizzed some of the leading neuroscientists about where they think future advances in brain science lie. These leaders identified half a dozen areas where they look forward to exciting developments.

The first is research into how memories are recorded and retrieved. As sometimes happens in other rapidly advancing scientific fields, developments in another field may hold the key to fresh advances. For example, fine-scale fMRI scans prompt leading researcher Eleanor Maguire to say, "We can actually now identify individual memory traces by the pattern of activity in areas of the brain such as the hippocampus. We can predict in an experiment the memory that someone is recalling."[6] But Greg Miller reminds us that "the choices are limited and that the technology is nowhere close to being able to read out any fleeting memory that crosses someone's mind."[7] You might ask, would it matter if they managed to find where some of our treasured religious memories are located? I don't think so. (Why should it matter to a Christian *where* spiritual experiences are embodied?) This is just another example of the ever-tightening links between mind and brain.

Another area in which the editors of *Science* look for advances is mental disease. Despite the 1950s excitement of drugs becoming available to help manage some forms of disease, solid advances since then have been disappointingly slow. Today there are encouraging signs, such as the use of deep brain stimulation that seems to help in some cases of depression.

There is in this field another encouraging trend. It comes from the comments of leading neurogeneticist Daniel Geschwind. Focusing on the continued efforts to understand autism, he writes:

> Gene expression profiling—investigating the activity of thousands of genes—in these human neurons could help researchers identify the biological pathways disrupted by autism risk genes and screen drugs to correct them. . . . I'm extremely optimistic that by using a combination of these methods we're going to develop new classes of drugs. . . . I think we're on the threshold of something really exciting.[8]

We share his excitement as we remember that not so very long ago some of the strange (to us) behavior of people with autism was interpreted by some religious people as being the result of indwelling by evil spirits.

Another current question: Why are our brains so big relative to our body size compared with other animals? Those who write about this often quote the important contribution by Richard Byrne, one of my colleagues here at St Andrews.[9] Richard and others like him, such as Robin Dunbar, speculate about why, for instance, the human brain is more than three times as large as that of the chimpanzee, our closest living evolutionary cousin.[10] Again, I don't see any religious stakes in this. As Christians we believe that, in a sense I spelled out some time ago, what makes us radically different is not merely something neuropsychological about us but who we are called to be.

Yet another question posed is: Why are you and your brain unique? Here again it seems that new brain imaging methods that highlight connections between brain regions could yield new clues about what makes each brain unique. But again, for us in the context of our Christian beliefs, it is persons who are unique, not only brains. We believe that we are uniquely offered the opportunity to enter into a personal relationship with our Creator God and uniquely called to responsible stewardship of his wonderful creation.

Yet another challenge is whether we can make our brains more plastic. And so we could go on, but in all these possible developments I do not see any particular stakes for Christians except, very importantly, as opportunities for those like you who are privileged to have the specialist training you are now getting. Here is a way for you and others like you to fulfill your calling to be part of the teams of dedicated researchers in cognitive neuroscience in order to help relieve suffering.

Several of these contributions by leaders in the field of brain science further remind us that there are similar rapid advances in psychology. The picture of psychological research as work in progress was underlined when Professor Francesca Happé gave the Rosalind Franklin Award Lecture at the Royal Society of London in October 2011. A leading researcher on autism, she reminded us, as we now know, that the neurodevelopmental condition is not caused by "refrigerator mothers," and that there is something different in the brains and genes of those with the autistic spectrum disorders.[11] But we don't know which part of the brain and we don't know how the relevant genes exert their effects. We need to recognize the heterogeneity of the condition, that none of the neurocognitive explanations can explain *all* the features of autism (it is not just "reduced ability to mind read"), and that we don't know why it is more prevalent in men than women. There is so much we don't know, but with patience and sustained effort there is hope for the future.

Malcolm,

When you mentioned your colleague Richard Byrne, that reminded me that you had written a good deal about the implications of developments in evolutionary psychology for our understanding of ourselves. Are there any developments on the horizon here that may present fresh challenges to widely accepted views about human nature?

Ben,

Another *Perspectives in Psychological Science* paper suggests one possible answer to that question. David Buss asks, "How Can Evolutionary Psychology Successfully Explain Personality and Individual Differences?"[12] This is another instance of how developments in one specialist area of psychology have implications for another. In this instance, developments in evolutionary psychology enrich the study of personality and individual differences.

Buss notes that some of the early leaders in this field regarded "heritable individual differences as what they described as 'noise' in the system and as irrelevant to the basic functioning of the psychological machinery."[13] He refers to Tooby and Cosmides, who in 1990 suggested that individual differences are "best viewed as 'noise' and are thus irrelevant to the basic functioning of the psychological machinery, much like differences in the colors of the wires of a car engine do not affect its basic functioning."[14] Buss agrees that this assumption was reasonable twenty years ago but believes that it is now seriously challenged by developments in evolutionary biology and advances in the evolutionary foundations of psychology. He believes that "one key toward a deeper understanding of personality and individual differences will come from changing the ways in which psychologists conceptualize them. . . . Specifically, at least some personality differences can be conceptualized as alternative strategies for solving recurrent adaptive problems."[15] Whether he is correct will be revealed by the results of further studies. Buss himself recognizes the problems we face for research in this area and concludes, "Although we are a long distance from answering the question of how to explain personality and individual differences, modern evolutionary psychology provides some powerful conceptual tools for doing so."[16] I think, in light of our earlier discussions, it further underlines what I have called the psychobiological unity of human beings.

Malcolm,

Given that anthropology deals with the science of understanding human beings, I'm surprised that at no point have you talked about what is going on at the interfaces between, for example, anthropology, evolutionary psychology and neuroscience. Are there any potential connections here that you know of?

Ben,

You aren't alone in wondering about the intersection of those fields. In "What Makes Us Human? Answers from Evolutionary Anthropology," influential scholars argue that:[17]

- *Humans are genetically akin to other species.* Human and chimp genomes are 99 percent identical. We are leaves on one tree.
- *Humans have an exceptional capacity for symbolic behavior, language and culture*—though, as we have seen, primates also exhibit some capacity for language and culture.
- *Humans have the most fully developed theory of mind.* We can think about thinking, and infer others' thinking.

Carrying the evolutionary perspective further, scholars are now speculating about an evolutionary psychology of religion. Religious thinking serves adaptive functions. It fosters morality, social cohesion and group survival. No wonder religion is so widespread. (When the Gallup World Poll asked humans across the planet "Is religion important in your daily life?" the global median proportion of adults who answered *yes* was 84 percent.[18])

For some devout Christians, that may set alarm bells ringing. Any suggestion that their capacity to believe in God and express that belief in sincere faith can be put under the microscope of cognitive scientists and evolutionary psychologists is a step too far. Their religious faith is something very precious and very special—how then could anyone suggest that it had just evolved?

Malcolm,

I'm not surprised that alarm bells have gone off for people of faith. Isn't it likely, given what's happened in the past, that such new knowledge will be used to explain away religion and avoid any of the moral or ethical demands of religion, assuming it is *true*?

Ben,

Fortunately, some of the leading scholars researching cognitive and evolutionary accounts of religion are committed Christians and are acknowledged by their peers, whether Christian or not, as careful researchers. One such is Justin Barrett, whom I mentioned before. In a forthcoming chapter, written with his colleague Matthew Jarvinen, he asks, "Do such accounts, then, undercut the theological claim that human personhood is specially marked as being *imago Dei*, in the image or likeness of God?"[19]

You will remember that we have several times talked about mind reading or theory of mind as described by cognitive psychologists and evolutionary psychologists. These authors believe that, in the course of evolution leading to the development of humans, this capacity for mind reading has developed significantly further. This further developed state they label *higher order theory of mind* (HO-ToM), and they write, "Whether nonhumans (or even humans before the age of three) have HO-ToM is unsettled. Far less controversial is that adult humans commonly exercise third-order intentionality, and we have no reason to think that any non-human species does so."[20] (I would add here a brief note of caution—no reason, maybe, on the evidence currently available, but evidence for it in nonhuman species may yet appear.)

They later add:

> An extra biblical, non-theological clue to the importance of HO-ToM as critical to *imago Dei* comes from cognitive science of religion (CSR). As a scientific study of religious thoughts and actions which draws upon the cognitive sciences and evolutionary psychology, CSR scholarship has begun to sound off on what cognitive mechanisms humans must have to conceptualize a god and to generate actions for interacting with that god. Recurrently, HO-ToM appears as a central player in these accounts.[21]

Barrett and his colleague point out that other leading researchers in this field argue that "religious rituals, then, are subtle extensions or small tweaks on ordinary ToM applied to human-super human interactions instead of human-human interactions."[22]

Another quote from Barrett and Jarvinen's forthcoming chapter illustrates well the relevance of this approach to the understanding of religion. They write,

> That is, the cognitive equipment that gives rise to religious expression is presumed to have evolved under selection pressures unrelated to religion or religious entities. Whereas the ease with which humans acquire fear of snakes

> presumably evolved in response to snakes themselves as a survival threat, the ease with which humans acquire belief in gods is not thought to have evolved in response to gods. Under these accounts religious thoughts are an evolutionary byproduct and not an adaptation per se.[23]

These authors squarely face the problem that this kind of research generates. They write, "For the sake of argument, let us suppose that the CSR-type account is broadly accurate. Does such an account, then, undercut or cast doubt on the theological claim that human personhood is specially marked as being *imago Dei*, in the image or likeness of God?"[24] They do not believe so. They continue, "For example, many things we regard as good, including art and music; many things we believe are truth producing, such as your favorite branch of mathematics or philosophy; and many things we value as useful, such as clothing and fishing tackle, are evolutionary byproducts in a comparable respect."[25] Indeed they note that Noam Chomsky recognized modern science as a possible evolutionary byproduct. And they point out that philosopher Peter van Invagen has observed that an evolutionary byproduct could very well be intentional and not an "accident" at all.[26] Referring to van Invagen's views, Barrett writes: "That is, God could have selected this universe out of any number of possible ones because it featured in one species a tendency toward theism as one (by)product of evolution."[27]

Malcolm,

It helps knowing that not just you, but other scientists such as Barrett, see no inherent conflict between evolution and faith. Moreover, I suppose that if science could seek to explain religion it could also seek to explain atheism (what leads some people to disbelieve?)—and a complete psychology of atheism would no more debunk atheism than a complete psychology of theism would debunk theism. Whether God exists or not is a separate question from why some people believe and others do not.

Ben,

We are indeed fortunate that some of the key players in these rapidly developing areas of research are Christian scholars and scientists. They are, as we might put it, down on the pitch in the middle of the rough-and-tumble of the game and not sitting up in the stands offering, at times, sadly uninformed comments about what seems to be happening in the arena. There is always the temptation to remain up in the stands, with preconceived ideas about how the game should be played, without being willing to acquaint oneself with the rules of the game and enter into the cut and thrust of what is actually happening. There is no doubt that on all of these issues where, I have suggested, rapid developments are occurring, we shall, at times, hear quick reactions based on presuppositions that need to be carefully re-examined, rather than well-informed comments, analyses and criticisms based on relevant evidence.

I suspect, then, that in the near future we are going to witness wider debate of some of the issues raised by ongoing research into the evolutionary origins of religion. With regard to this issue, as well as the others I mentioned earlier, as we witness rapidly developing knowledge, this may cause understandable concern amongst some serious Christians. In such circumstances there remains the danger of knee-jerk reactions that may be less than helpful. Sadly, it is possible, faced with the seemingly relentless incoming tide of developing science and some of its wider implications, to see them as a threat to our understandably treasured Christian beliefs. Viewed in this way, the danger is that some Christians rush around frantically filling more sandbags to stem the incoming tide of knowledge.

I suggest we should rather view the incoming tide as a potential source of help enabling us to discard the litter of outdated and inaccurate knowledge. I would suggest that if we remember that the God we worship is, as we are taught in Scripture, the Creator and Sustainer of all that is, then the knowledge that our God chooses to give us through Scripture cannot ultimately conflict with the knowledge he chooses to give us by using the minds he has given us to understand his universe. Since we believe that God is the author of all truth, the accounts from the two sources will ultimately not conflict, though there will be many puzzles and much hard thinking along the way. This means that we should welcome the incoming tide of knowledge, giving us new insights into the wonders of the creation of which we are a part, and a deeper understanding of how, as Scripture teaches, we are "fearfully and wonderfully made" (Psalm 139:14).

Appendix

Scripture Union International Statement of Hermeneutical Principles

Scripture Union has adopted the following hermeneutical principles for use by editors, writers and all who handle the Bible on behalf of the movement.

Rather than being seen as options on a menu, these principles are to be taken as a whole; and taken together, they are to govern our approach every time we come to Scripture. The emphasis placed on each one may vary on different occasions, but all should be informing our thinking, at least implicitly.

We believe that the Bible should be interpreted:

a. Prayerfully, in humility and in dependence on the Holy Spirit. We come to Scripture acknowledging that only the Holy Spirit can open our blind eyes and illumine our dark hearts to what God is saying. As God's empowering presence, the Spirit will lead people to engage with the text and to face God's challenge in the here and now. The recognition that the Holy Spirit brings a sense of immediacy will draw us into an understanding, not just of the original meaning of the text, but also of its contemporary prophetic significance.

b. Corporately rather than simply individualistically. We are the body of Christ. We stand in a line of historical interpretation that we respect, and from which we learn. As we engage with Scripture together, greater understanding emerges, fellowship is deepened and appropriation encouraged.

c. As a whole. We are committed to the whole of Scripture, to allowing Scripture to interpret Scripture, and to promoting the understanding of the broad sweep of God's dealings with humanity from creation to new creation. In doing this we affirm that the Bible is a metanarrative; that is, it tells a story which gives meaning to all of life, and by which all of life must be judged. In terms of this metanarrative, we will emphasize interpretation both as propositional and as a response to this metanarrative, and help people to enter imaginatively into the biblical story, seeking always to lead them to live under its authority.

d. Contextually—as it was written. The Bible contains different literary forms (genres) and the way God communicates often differs from one to another. Therefore interpretation includes recognizing and respecting the genre of each passage. The passage is then to be interpreted according to the author's intention and in terms of its historical and canonical context. To the criticism that, however desirable this may be, it is unattainable, we assert that, while exhaustive knowledge of these things may be impossible, adequate knowledge is not.

e. Contextually—as it is encountered. Our presuppositions, culture, gender, age, and personal history—in short, all that is going on in our lives and communities—always color our encounter with Scripture. Every encounter is an interpretation. Nevertheless we can know and experience scriptural truth; and while our communities exercise a significant influence on our understanding of Scripture, they are not ultimately a binding force. We need constantly to bring our understanding of Scripture back to Scripture. At the same time we need to listen to the interpretation of Scripture of others who belong to different contexts, so that our understanding may be enriched and our blind spots corrected.

f. Contextually—as it is lived out. Encountering God through his Word will have an impact on our lives, encouraging us in worship, mission, and holiness. As we commit ourselves to obeying God's Word, our experience will help us to understand the Bible better, and deepen our faith in, and our fellowship with, God.

g. Christologically. Jesus Christ (his birth and life on earth, his death and resurrection, his ascension and second coming) is God's key Word in his dealings with human beings; and he, therefore, is the focus of God's revelation in the Bible. Our basic aim states that meeting God through the Bible and prayer will lead to personal faith in Christ. The Holy Spirit leads us into the truth, always testifying to and glorifying Jesus. In the light of these things, in engaging with the Bible, we should consider how a passage ultimately relates to Jesus Christ.

h. Relationally: a meeting with God. We do not read the Bible simply to collect information about God. Rather, through the stories, promises, commands, warnings and examples, we begin to understand God, meet with him and know him personally. To attempt to interpret Scripture and yet somehow to stop short of enjoying that relationship of love, is to miss the entire purpose for which God, whose nature is love, has revealed himself in the Bible. God is a relational God, his character is to build and sustain relationships. So all our interpretation of Scripture is to be rooted in the two dimensions of our relatedness to God as his children, and of the web of human relationships around us.

Fundamentally, engaging with the Bible is about a relationship with God, and this can only be achieved by dependence on the Holy Spirit.

Further Reading

Preface

Davis, E. B. "Robert Boyle's Religious Life, Attitudes, and Vocation." *Science and Christian Belief* 19, no. 2 (2007): 117-38.

Hooykaas, R. *Robert Boyle: A Study in Science and Christian Belief.* Lanham, Md.: University of America Press, 1997.

Jeeves, Malcolm. "Psychologising and Neurologising about Religion: Facts, Fallacies and the Future." *Science and Christian Belief* 21, no. 1 (2009): 25-54.

———. "What Does an Experimental Psychologist Mean When He Says 'I Know Jesus Christ.'" *HIS Magazine* (1954): 20-29.

1 What Is Psychology, and How Should We Approach It?

"Challenges and Priorities for Global Mental Health Research in Low- and Middle-Income Countries." Symposium Report of the Academy of Medical Sciences, December 2008.

Llibre Rodriguez, Juan J., et al. "Prevalence of Dementia in Latin America, India and China: A Population Based Cross-Sectional Survey." *Lancet* 372, no. 9637 (2008): 464-74.

———. "The Prevalence, Correlates and Impact of Dementia in Cuba: A 10/66 Group Population-Based Survey." *Neuroepidemiology* 31, no. 4 (2008): 243-51.

2 What Is the Relationship Between the Mind and the Brain?

Myers, David G. "The Biology of Mind." In *Psychology.* 9th ed. New York: Worth, 2009.

Sperry, R. W. "Mind, Brain, and Humanist Values." *Bulletin of the Atomic Scientists* 22, no. 7 (1966): 2-6.

———. "Psychology's Mentalist Paradigm and the Religion/Science Tension." *American Psychologist* 43, no. 8 (1988): 607-13.

3 How Free Am I? *Free Will and Determinism*

Murphy, Nancey, and Warren S. Brown. *Did My Neurons Make Me Do It?: Philosophical and Neurobiological Perspectives on Moral Responsibility and Free Will.* Oxford: Oxford University Press, 2007.

4 Determinism, Genetics and the "God Gene"

Boomsma, Dorret, et al., "A Religious Upbringing Reduces the Influence of Genetic Factors on Disinhibition: Evidence for the Interaction Between Genotype and Environment in Personality." *Twin Research* 2 (1999): 115-25.

Hamer, D. *The God Gene: How Faith Is Hard Wired into Our Genes*. New York: Doubleday, 2004.

Looy, Heather. "The Body of Faith: Genetic and Evolutionary Considerations." *Journal of Psychology and Christianity* 24, no. 2 (2005): 113-21.

McCall Smith, Alexander. "A Wee Identity Crisis." *New York Times*. March 11, 2007.

Wade, Nicholas. *The Faith Instinct*. New York: Penguin, 2009.

5 Have Benjamin Libet's Experiments Exploded the Free-Will Myth?

Gomes, Gilberto. "The Interpretation of Libet's Results on the Timing of Conscious Events: A Commentary." *Consciousness and Cognition* 11 (2002): 221-30.

Hallett, Mark. "Volitional Control of Movement: The Physiology of Free Will." *Clinical Neurophysiology* 118, no. 6 (2007): 1179-92.

Libet, B. "Do We Have Freewill?" *Journal of Consciousness Studies* 9 (1999): 47-57.

———. "Unconscious Cerebral Initiative and the Role of Conscious Will in Voluntary Action." *Behavioural and Brain Sciences* 8, no. 4 (1985): 529-66.

Libet, B., C. A. Gleason, E. W. Wright and D. K. Pearl. "Time of Conscious Intention to Act in Relation to Onset of Cerebral Activity (Readiness-Potential): The Unconscious Initiation of a Free Voluntary Act." *Brain* 106, no. 3 (1983): 623-42.

Obhi, S. S., and P. Haggard. "Freewill and Freewon't." *American Scientist* 923 (2004): 358-65.

Trevena, Judy, and Jeff Miller. "Cortical Movement Preparation Before and After a Conscious Decision to Move." *Consciousness and Cognition* 10, no. 2 (2002): 162-90.

6 But Is It All in the Brain? *The Emergence of Social Neuroscience*

Baumeister, Roy F. "Emergence of Personhood: Lessons from Self and Identity." In *The Emergence of Personhood: A Quantum Leap?* edited by Malcolm Jeeves. Eerdmans, forthcoming.

Cacioppo, J. *Foundations of Social Neuroscience*. Cambridge, Mass.: MIT Press, 2001.

Frith, Christopher D., and Daniel M. Wolpert. *The Neuroscience of Social Interaction: Decoding, Imitating, and Influencing the Actions of Others*. Oxford: Oxford University Press, 2004.

7 But What About the Soul?

Berry, R. J., and Malcolm Jeeves. "The Nature of Human Nature." *Science and Christian Belief* 20, no. 1 (2008): 3-47.

Eccles, John C. "Do Mental Events Cause Neural Events Analogously to the Probability Fields of Quantum Mechanics?" *Proceedings of the Royal Society of London, Series B* 227 (May 1986): 411-28.

———. *Evolution of the Brain: Creation of the Self*. London: Routledge, 1989.

Jeeves, Malcolm A. "Human Nature Without a Soul?" *European Review* 12 (February 2004): 45-64.

———. "Mind Reading and Soul Searching in the Twenty-First Century: The Scientific Evidence." In *What About the Soul?* Edited by Joel B. Green. Nashville: Abingdon Press, 2004.

Kidner, Derek. *Genesis: An Introduction and Commentary*. Downers Grove, Ill.: IVP Academic, 2008.

Popper, Karl R., and John C. Eccles. *The Self and Its Brain*. New York: Springer-Verlag, 1985.

Thistleton, Anthony C. "Human Personhood and the Image of God: A Contribution from Biblical and Christian Theology." In *The Emergence of Personhood: A Quantum Leap?* Edited by Malcolm Jeeves. Eerdmans, forthcoming.

9 What Makes Us Human? *The Development of Evolutionary Psychology*

Dunbar, Robin. *The Human Story*. London: Faber and Faber, 2004.

Tattersall, Ian. *Becoming Human: Evolution and Human Uniqueness*. Oxford: Oxford University Press, 1998.

10 Are Humans Different? *What About Morality in Animals?*

Gazzaniga, Michael S. *The Ethical Brain*. New York: Dana Press, 2005.

———. *Human: The Science Behind What Makes Us Unique*. New York: Harper Collins, 2008.

Muller, Corsin A., and Michael A. Cant. "Imitation and Traditions in Wild Banded Mongooses." *Current Biology* 20 (July 13, 2010): 1171-75.

11 What Is the Difference Between Altruism, Altruistic Love and Agape?

Emmons, Robert A., and Michael E. McCullough, eds. *The Psychology of Gratitude*. New York: Oxford University Press, 2004.

Post, Stephen G., Lynn G. Underwood, Jeffrey P. Schloss and William B. Hurlbut. *Altruism and Altruistic Love: Science, Philosophy & Religion in Dialogue*. Oxford: Oxford University Press, 2002.

12 Does Language Uniquely Define Us as Humans?

Arnold, Kate, and Klaus Zuberbuhler. "Call Combinations in Monkeys: Compositional or Idiomatic Expressions?" *Brain and Language* 120 (2012): 303-9.

Arnold, Kate, Yvonne Pohlner and Klaus Zuberbuhler. "Not Words but Meanings? Alarm Calling Behaviour in a Forest Guenon." In *Primates of Gashaka: Socioecology and Conservation in Nigeria's Biodiversity Hotspot*. Edited by Volker Sommer and Caroline Ross. New York: Springer, 2011.

Bouchet, H., C. Blois-Heulin, A. Pellier, K. Zuberbuhler and A. Lemasson. "Acoustic

Variability and Individual Distinctiveness in the Vocal Repertoire of Red-Capped Mangabeys (Cercocebus torquatus)." *Journal of Comparative Psychology* 126, no. 1 (February 2012): 45-56.

Byrne, R. W. "The Dividing Line: What Sets Humans Apart from Our Closest Relatives?" In *The Emergence of Personhood: A Quantum Leap?* Edited by Malcolm Jeeves. Eerdmans, forthcoming.

Zuberbuhler, Klaus, Kate Arnold and Katie Slocombe. "Living Links to Human Language." *In Primate Communication and Human Language: Vocalisation, Gestures, Imitation and Deixis in Humans and Non-Humans.* Edited by Anne Vilain, Jean-Luc Schwartz, Christian Abry and Jacques Vauclair. Amsterdam: John Benjamins, 2011.

Zuberbuhler, Klaus, and Roman M. Wittig. "Field Experiments with Non-human Primates: A Tutorial." In *Field and Laboratory Methods in Primatology: A Practical Guide.* Edited by Joanna M. Setchell and Deborah J. Curtis. Cambridge: Cambridge University Press, 2011.

13 Does My Brain Have a "God Spot"?

Johnstone, Brick, and Bret A. Glass. "Support for a Neuropsychological Model of Spirituality in Persons with Traumatic Brain Injury." *Zygon* 43 (December 2008): 861-74.

16 Are Religious Beliefs the Twenty-First-Century Opium of the People? *What About Placebo Effects?*

Beauregard, M. *The Spiritual Brain: A Neuroscientist's Case for the Existence of the Soul.* New York: HarperOne, 2007.

Beauregard, M., J. Lévesque and P. Bourgouin. "Neural Correlates of Conscious Self-Regulation of Emotion." *Journal of Neuroscience* 21 (September 2001): 6993-7000.

Beauregard, M., J. Lévesque and V. Paquette. "Neural Basis of Conscious and Voluntary Self-Regulation of Emotion." In *Consciousness, Emotional Self-Regulation and the Brain.* Edited by M. Beauregard. Amsterdam: John Benjamins, 2004.

Beauregard, M., and V. Paquette. "Neural Correlates of a Mystical Experience in Carmelite Nuns." *Neuroscience Letters* 405 (2006): 186-90.

Beauregard, M., V. Paquette, M. Pouliot and J. Lévesque. "The Neurobiology of the Mystical Experience: A Quantitative EEG Study." Society for Neuroscience 34th Annual Meeting, October 23-27, 2004, San Diego.

Fields, Howard L. "How the Nervous System Transforms Meaning into Bodily Healing." In *Spiritual Healing: Science, Meaning and Discernment.* Edited by Sarah Coakley. Grand Rapids: Eerdmans, 2012.

Harrington, Anne. *The Cure Within: A History of Mind-Body Medicine.* New York:

Norton, 2011.

Myers, David G. "National Secularity, Individual Religiosity, and Human Flourishing." *Perspectives* (August/September 2009).

———. *A Friendly Letter to Skeptics and Atheists: Musings on Why God Is Good and Faith Isn't Evil.* San Francisco: Jossey-Bass, 2008.

18 Can Science "Explain Away" Religion?

Dawes, Robyn M. *House of Cards: Psychology and Psychotherapy Built on Myth.* New York: Free Press, 1994.

Gross, Paul R., and Norman Levitt. *Higher Superstition.* Baltimore: Johns Hopkins University Press, 1994.

Jeeves, Malcolm, and Warren S. Brown. *Neuroscience, Psychology, and Religion: Illusions, Delusions, and Realities about Human Nature.* Templeton Science and Religion Series. West Conshohocken, Penn.: Templeton Press, 2009.

19 Where Next?

Jeeves, Malcolm. "Concluding Reflections." In *Cognitive Approaches to the Evolution of Religion: Critical Approaches.* Edited by Fraser Watts and Leon Turner. Oxford: Oxford University Press, forthcoming.

Notes

Preface

[1]J. J. MacIntosh and Peter Anstey, "Robert Boyle," in the *Stanford Encyclopedia of Philosophy,* Fall 2007 <http://plato.Stanford.edu/archives/fall2007/entries/boyle/>.

[2]John Stott, *Through the Bible, Through the Year* (Grand Rapids: Baker, 2006), p. 370.

[3]Mark Noll, *Jesus Christ and the Life of the Mind* (Grand Rapids: Eerdmans, 2011), p. x.

[4]Christopher Bugbee, "A Higher Purpose for Higher Education," *Milestones*, John Templeton Foundation, June 2005 <www.templeton.org>.

[5]Malcolm Jeeves, ed., *Human Nature,* based on a conference at the Royal Society of Edinburgh (Edinburgh: The Royal Society of Edinburgh, 2006); Jeeves, ed., *From Cells to Souls—and Beyond: Changing Portraits of Human Nature* (Grand Rapids: Eerdmans, 2004); Jeeves, ed., *Rethinking Human Nature: A Multidisciplinary Approach* (Grand Rapids: Eerdmans, 2011); Jeeves, ed., *The Emergence of Personhood: A Quantum Leap?* (Grand Rapids: Eerdmans, forthcoming).

[6]Malcolm Jeeves, "Not All Herrings Are Red," *HIS Magazine* (February 1959): 11-15.

[7]David Smith, *Moving Toward Emmaus: Hope in a Time of Uncertainty* (London: SPCK, 2007), pp. 60-61, italics mine.

[8]Ibid., p. 61.

[9]International Fellowship of Evangelical Students, prayer letter, 2011.

[10]Stott, *Through the Bible,* p. 370.

[11]Tom Wright, *Paul for Everyone: The Prison Letters*, 2nd ed. (Louisville: SPCK/Westminster John Knox, 2004), p. 51.

[12]C. S. Lewis, *Letters to Malcolm: Chiefly on Prayer* (London: Geoffrey Bles, 1964).

1 What Is Psychology, and How Should We Approach It?

[1]David G. Myers, *Psychology,* 9th ed. (New York: Worth Publishers, 2010).

[2]Howard Gardner, *The Mind's New Science: A History of the Cognitive Revolution* (New York: Basic Books, 1985), p. 29.

[3]Marilyn S. Albert, "The Science of the Mind," *Science* 275 (March 1997): 1547.

[4]Paul Vitello, "George A. Miller, a Pioneer in Cognitive Psychology, Is Dead at 92," *New York Times,* August 1, 2012 <http://www.nytimes.com/2012/08/02/us/george-a-miller-cognitive-psychology-pioneer-dies-at-92.html?_r=1&pagewanted=all>.

[5]Sabine Bahn, "New Blood-Test to Aid in Schizophrenia Diagnosis," University of Cambridge Research News, June 28, 2010 <http://www.cam.ac.uk/research/news/new-blood-test-to-aid-in-schizophrenia-diagnosis/>.

[6]"Challenges and Priorities for Global Mental Health Research in Low- and Middle-Income Countries," Symposium Report, The Academy of Medical Sciences, December 2008.

[7]Martin Rees, "Keeping it Real: The Art of Science," in *Eureka*, supplement to *The Times* (October 2009): 9.

[8]Michael Atiya, interviewed by Ronald Kerr.

[9]Charles Darwin, *A Biographical Sketch of an Infant,* 1877.

[10]Eric L. Johnson, ed., *Psychology & Christianity: Five Views* 2nd ed. (Downers Grove, Ill.: InterVarsity Press, 2010).

2 What Is the Relationship Between the Mind and the Brain?

[1]John Stein, "The Most Important Problems in Neuroscience," *The Psychologist* 24 (December 2011): 870-71.

[2]Ibid.

[3]Carol R. Albright and James B. Ashbrook, *Where God Lives in the Human Brain* (Naperville, Ill.: Sourcebooks, 2001).

[4]Andrew Newberg and Mark R. Waldman, *How God Changes Your Brain* (New York: Ballantine Books, 2009).

[5]David G. Myers and Malcolm A. Jeeves, *Psychology Through the Eyes of Faith*, 2nd ed. (San Francisco: HarperSanFrancisco, 2003).

[6]David G. Myers, "The Biology of Mind," in *Psychology*, 9th ed. (New York: Worth Publishers, 2010).

[7]N. T. Wright, personal communication, April 2012.

[8]Randy L. Buchner, Jessica R. Andrews-Hanna and Daniel L. Schacter, "The Brain's Default Network: Anatomy, Function, and Relevance to Disease," *Annals of the New York Academy of Sciences* 1124 (2008): 1.

[9]Gregoire Borst, William L. Thompson and Stephen M. Kosslyn, "Understanding the Dorsal and Ventral Systems of the Human Cerebral Cortex: Beyond Dichotomies," *The American Psychologist* 66 (October 2011): 624.

[10]Iain McGilchrist, *The Master and His Emissary: The Divided Brain and the Making of the Western World* (New Haven: Yale University Press, 2010).

[11]N. T. Wright, "Imagining the Kingdom: Mission and Theology in Early Christianity," *Scottish Journal of Theology*, in press.

[12]Arthur W. Toga and Paul M. Thompson, "Mapping Brain Asymmetry," *Nature Reviews Neuroscience* 4 (January 2003): 37-48.

[13]Borst, Thompson and Kosslyn, "Understanding the Dorsal and Ventral Systems," p. 624, italics mine.

[14]Ibid.

[15]Roger Sperry, in R. L. Gregory, ed., *The Oxford Companion to the Mind* (Oxford: Oxford University Press, 1987), pp. 164-65.

[16]Thomas Nagel, "Science and the Mind-Body Problem," in *What Is Our Real Knowledge About the Human Being?* (Vatican City: Pontifica Academia Scientiarum, 2007), pp. 96-100.

[17]Raymond Tallis, *Aping Mankind: Neuromania, Darwinitis, and the Misrepresentation of Humanity* (Durham, UK: Acumen Publishing, 2011).

[18]Carol A. Tavris, "Debunking Pseudoneuroscience," David Myers Distinguished Lecture on the Science and Craft of Teaching Psychology, Association for Psychological Science, May 25, 2012, Chicago.

[19]Antonio Damasio, *Descartes' Error: Emotion, Reason, and the Human Brain* (New York: Putnam, 1994).

[20]Robert E. Kendell, "The Distinction Between Mental and Physical Illness," *British Journal of Psychiatry* 178 (2001): 490-93.

[21]Eleanor A. Maguire et al., "Navigation–Related Structural Change in the Hippocampi of Taxi Drivers," *Proceedings of the National Academy of Sciences* 97 (April 11, 2000): 4398-403.

[22]Katherine Woollett and Eleanor A. Maguire, "Acquiring 'the Knowledge' of London's Layout Drives Structural Brain Changes," *Current Biology* 21 (December 2011): 2109-114.

[23]Vincent Paquette et al., "Change the Mind and You Change the Brain: Effects of Cognitive-Behaviour Therapy on the Neural Correlates of Spider Phobia," *NeuroImage* 18 (2003): 401-9.

3 How Free Am I? *Free Will and Determinism*

[1]Professor Nicholas Mackintosh FRS, "Brain Waves Module 4: Neuroscience and the Law," report on the National Academy of Sciences Sackler Forum, December 13, 2011 <http//royalsociety.org/policy/projects/brain-waves/responsibility-law/>.

[2]MacArthur Foundation New Scientist Report, December 14, 2011 <http://www.macfound.org/press/speeches/announcement-law-and-neuroscience-project-jonathan-fanton-federal-court-house-new-york-ny-october-9-2007/>.

[3]"fMRI Evidence in Court: Summary of *Nature* Paper on Revised Judgment on Stefanini Albertani," *The Psychologist* 24 (October 10, 2011).

[4]Daniel T. Tranel, quoted by Chris Kahn in "Paedophile 'Cured' After Surgery," reported by the Associated Press, July 28, 2003.

[5]Peter Clarke, "Neuroscience and the Soul: A Response to Malcolm Jeeves," *Science and Christian Belief* 21 (April 2009): 61-64.

4 Determinism, Genetics and the "God Gene"

[1]David G. Myers, "Nature, Nurture, and Human Diversity," in *Psychology*, 9th ed. (New York: Worth Publishers, 2010), pp. 133-72.

[2]Stephen J. Gould, "Message from a Mouse," *New York Times*, September 13, 1999, p. 64.

[3]Daniel Geschwind, quoted in Perri Klass, "On the Left Hand, There Are No Easy Answers," *New York Times*, March 6, 2011 <http://www.nytimes.com/2011/03/08/health/views/08klass.html?_r=1>.

[4]L. J. Eaves et al., "Comparing the Biological and Cultural Inheritance of Personality and Social Attitudes in the Virginia 30,000 Study of Twins and Their Relatives," *Twin Research* 2 (1999): 62-80.

[5]Lindon Eaves, "Genetic and Social Influences on Religion and Values," in *From Cells to Souls—and Beyond*, ed. Malcolm Jeeves (Grand Rapids: Eerdmans, 2004), p. 108.

[6]Ibid., p. 112.

[7]Ibid., p. 111.

[8]Dorret Boomsma et al., "A Religious Upbringing Reduces the Influence of Genetic Factors on Disinhibition: Evidence for the Interaction Between Genotype and Environment in Personality," *Twin Research* 2 (1999): 115-25.

[9]John Horgan, "Do Our Genes Influence Behavior? Why We Want to Think They Do," *Chronicle of Higher Education*, November 26, 2004 <http://chronicle.com/article/Do-Our-Genes-Influence/21999/>.

[10]Laura B. Koenig, Matt McGue, Robert Krueger and Thomas J. Bouchard Jr., "Genetic and Environmental Influences on Religiousness: Findings for Retrospective and Current Religiousness Ratings," *Journal of Personality* 73 (April 2005): 471-88.

5 Have Benjamin Libet's Experiments Exploded the Free-Will Myth?

[1]Benjamin Libet, E. W. Wright Jr. and G. A. Gleason, "Readiness-Potentials Preceding Unre-

stricted 'Spontaneous' vs. Preplanned Voluntary Acts," *Electroencephalography and Clinical Neurophysiology* 54 (1982): 322-35.

[2]Benjamin Libet, "Unconscious Cerebral Initiative and the Role of Conscious Will in Voluntary Action," *Behavioral and Brain Sciences* 8 (1985): 536.

[3]Masao Matsuhashi and Mark Hallett, "The Timing of the Conscious Intention to Move," *European Journal of Neuroscience* 28 (2008): 2344-51.

[4]Ibid., p. 2344.

[5]Jeff Miller, Peter Shepherdson and Judy Trevena, "Effects of Clock Monitoring on Electroencephalographic Activity: Is Unconscious Movement Initiation an Artifact of the Clock?" *Psychological Science* 22 (January 2011): 103-9.

[6]Ibid., p. 107.

[7]M. Brass and P. Haggard, "The What, When, and Whether Model of Intentional Action," *The Neuroscientist* 14 (2008): 323.

[8]Mark Hallett, "Volitional Control of Movement: The Physiology of Free Will," *Clinical Neurophysiology* 118 (June 2007): 1179-92.

[9]Ibid., p. 1182.

[10]Ibid., p. 1192.

[11]Hannah Tepper, "The Controversial Science of Free Will," *Salon*, November 13, 2011 <http://www.salon.com/2011/11/13/the_controversial_science_of_free_will/>.

[12]Ibid.

[13]Benedict Carey, "Decoding the Brain's Cacophony," *New York Times*, October 31, 2011 <http://www.nytimes.com/2011/11/01/science/telling-the-story-of-the-brains-cacophony-of-competing-voices.html?pagewanted=all&_r=0>.

[14]Aaron Schurger, Jacobo D. Sitt and Stanislas Dehaene, "An Accumulator Model for Spontaneous Neural Activity Prior to Self-Initiated Movement," *Proceedings of the National Academy of Sciences* (August 2012), quoted in Anil Ananthaswamy, "Brain May Not Stand in the Way of Free Will," *New Scientist*, August 8, 2012.

[15]Ibid., italics mine.

[16]Seth Anil, quoted in Ananthaswamy, "Brain May Not Stand in the Way of Free Will."

6 But Is It All in the Brain? *The Emergence of Social Neuroscience*

[1]Chris Frith and Daniel Wolpert, *The Neuroscience of Social Interaction* (New York: Oxford University Press, 2004).

[2]John T. Cacioppo and Gary G. Berntson, eds., *Social Neuroscience* (New York: Psychology Press, 2005).

[3]Ibid., p. xiii.

[4]Ibid., p. 7.

[5]Ibid., p. 239.

[6]Ibid., p. 241, italics mine.

[7]S. S. Stevens, *Handbook of Experimental Psychology* (New York: Wiley, 1951).

[8]David G. Myers, *Intuition: Its Powers and Perils* (London and New Haven, Conn.: Yale University Press, 2002), p. 322.

[9]Robert Emmons, "Religion and Personality," in *Handbook of Religion and Mental Health*, ed. H. G. Koenig (San Diego: Academic Press, 2001).

[10]Roy F. Baumeister, E. J. Masicampo and Kathleen Vohs, “Do Conscious Thoughts Cause Behavior?” in *Annual Review of Psychology* 62 (2011): 331-61.

7 But What About the Soul?

[1]Chris Frith, “Making Up the Mind,” *The Psychologist* 22 (October 2009): 842-45.

[2]James Barr, *Biblical Faith and Natural Theology* (Oxford, UK: Clarendon, 1993).

[3]Joel B. Green, *Body, Soul, and Human Life: The Nature of Humanity in the Bible* (Grand Rapids: Baker Academic, 2008), p. 53.

[4]Anthony C. Thiselton, “The Image and Likeness of God: A Theological Approach,” in *The Emergence of Personhood: A Quantum Leap?*, ed. Malcolm Jeeves (Grand Rapids: Eerdmans, forthcoming).

[5]N. T. Wright, reflections on what it means to be human, personal communication, June 17, 2011.

[6]James L. Wright, “The Mortal Soul in Ancient Israel and Pauline Christianity: Ramifications for Modern Medicine,” *Journal of Religion and Health* 50 (June 2011): 447-51.

[7]Lawson G. Stone, “The Soul: Possession, Part or Person? The Genesis of Human Nature in Genesis 2:7,” in *What About the Soul: Neuroscience and Christian Anthropology*, ed. Joel B. Green (Nashville: Abingdon Press, 2004), pp. 47-62.

[8]H. D. McDonald, *The Christian View of Man* (London: Marshall, Morgan and Scott, 1981).

[9]See, for example, Peter Enns, *Inspiration and Incarnation: Evangelicals and the Problem of the Old Testament* (Grand Rapids: Baker Academic, 2005); Enns, *The Evolution of Adam* (Grand Rapids: Brazos, 2012).

[10]John R. W. Stott, *The Message of Romans* (Downers Grove, Ill.: InterVarsity Press, 1994), p. 223.

[11]Ibid., p. 224.

[12]Derek Kidner, “Introduction,” in *Commentary on Psalms 1-72* (Downers Grove, Ill.: Inter-Varsity Press, 1973), p. 1.

[13]Ibid., p. 65, italics mine.

[14]A. F. Walls, “Soul,” in *New Bible Dictionary*, 2nd ed. (Leicester, U.K.: Inter-Varsity Press, 1982), pp. 1135-36.

[15]Patrick D. Miller, “What Is a Human Being? The Anthropology of Scripture,” in *What About the Soul: Neuroscience and Christian Anthropology*, ed. Joel B. Green (Nashville: Abingdon, 2004), p. 72.

[16]Joel B. Green and Stuart L. Palmer, eds., *In Search of the Soul: Four Views of the Mind-Body Problem* (Downers Grove, Ill.: InterVarsity Press, 2005).

[17]Enns, *Inspiration and Incarnation*, p. 55.

[18]Mark A. Noll, *Jesus Christ and the Life of the Mind* (Grand Rapids: Eerdmans, 2011), p. 180.

[19]J. Harold Ellens and Wayne G. Rollins, *Psychology and the Bible: A New Way to Read the Scriptures* (Westport, Conn.: Praeger, 2004).

[20]Fraser Watts, “Approaching the Gospels Psychologically,” in *Jesus and Psychology*, ed. Watts (Philadelphia: Templeton, 2007), p. 4.

[21]Richard Bauckham, *Jesus and the Eyewitnesses: The Gospels as Eyewitness Testimony* (Grand Rapids: Eerdmans, 2007).

[22]Joanna Collicutt, “Bringing the Academic Discipline of Psychology to Bear on the Study of the Bible,” *The Journal of Theological Studies*, n.s. 63 (April 2012): 48.

[23]George A. Marsden, *Jonathan Edwards: A Life* (New Haven, Conn.: Yale University Press, 2003), p. 474.

[24]N. T. Wright, *Scripture and the Authority of God: How to Read the Bible Today* (London: SPCK, 2005).

8 Don't Parapsychology and Near-Death Experiences Prove the Existence of the Soul?

[1]Rhea White, "Intuition, Heart Knowledge, and Parapsychology," *Journal of the American Society for Psychical Research,* 92 (1998): 150-71.

[2]Samuel Mouton and Stephen Kosslyn, "Using Neuroimaging to Resolve the Psi Debate," *Journal of Cognitive Neuroscience* 20 (2008): 182-92.

[3]David G. Myers, *Psychology,* 9th ed. (New York: Worth Publishers, 2010), pp. 238-88, "Putting ESP to Experimental Test."

[4]Ibid., p. 126.

[5]Ibid., p. 126.

[6]Joel B. Green, "Resurrection of the Body: New Testament Voices Concerning Personal Continuity and the After Life," in *What About the Soul?* ed. Joel B. Green (Nashville: Abingdon, 2004), p. 95.

[7]Andrew Newberg and Mark R. Waldman, *How God Changes Your Brain* (New York: Ballantine Books, 2009).

[8]Henrick H. Ehrsson, "The Experimental Induction of Out-of-the-Body Experiences," *Science* 317 (2007): 1048.

[9]Olaf Blanke, T. Landis, L. Spinelli and M. Seeck, "Out-of-Body Experience and Autoscopy of Neurological Origin," *Brain* 127 (2): 243-58.

[10]Bill T. Arnold, "Soul-Searching Questions About 1 Samuel 28: Samuel's Appearance at Endor and Christian Anthropology," in *What About the Soul?* ed. Joel B. Green (Nashville: Abingdon, 2004).

[11]Ibid., p. 78.

[12]Ibid., p. 81.

9 What Makes Us Human? *The Development of Evolutionary Psychology*

[1]Leda Cosmides and John Tooby, "Cognitive Adaptations for Social Change," in J. Berkov, L. Cosmides and J. Tooby (eds.), *The Adapted Mind: Evolutionary Psychology and the Generation of Culture* (New York: Oxford University Press, 1992), p. 7.

[2]Frans de Waal, *Good Natured: The Origin of Right and Wrong in Humans and Other Animals* (Cambridge, Mass.: Harvard, 1997).

[3]Blaise Pascal, *Pensees* (1659).

[4]David Buss, *Evolutionary Psychology: The New Science of the Mind* (Boston: Pearson Education, 2000).

[5]Robin Dunbar, "Taking Evolutionary Psychology Seriously," *The Psychologist* 21 (April 2008): 304.

[6]Ibid.

[7]Ibid.

[8]Ibid.

[9]D. G. Premack and G. Woodruff, "Does the Chimpanzee Have a Theory of Mind?" *Behavioural and Brain Sciences* 1 (1978): 515-26.

[10]A. Whiten, "Theory of Mind," in *Encyclopedia of Cognitive Science*, ed. L. Nadel, vol. 4 (London: Nature Publishing Group, 2005), pp. 376-79.

[11]Ibid., p. 377.

[12]Michael Tomasello, J. Call and B. Hare, "Chimpanzees Understand Psychological States—The Question Is Which Ones and to What Extent," *Trends in Cognitive Science* 7 (2003): 153-56.

[13]Michael Tomasello and E. Herman, "Ape and Human Cognition: What's the Difference?" *Current Directions in Psychological Research* 19 (2010): 3-8.

[14]Richard Byrne, "Evolutionary Psychology and Socio-Biology: Prospects and Dangers," in *Human Nature*, ed. Malcolm Jeeves (Edinburgh: Royal Society of Edinburgh, 2006), pp. 84-105.

[15]Academy of Medical Sciences, "Animals Containing Human Material," July 2011 <http://www.acmedsci.ac.uk/p47prid77.html>.

[16]Ibid., p. 48 of full report.

[17]Francis Crick, *The Astonishing Hypothesis: The Scientific Search for the Soul* (New York: Simon & Schuster, 1994), p. 3.

[18]Ibid., p. 261.

10 Are Humans Different? *What About Morality in Animals?*

[1]Andrew Whiten, Victoria Horner and Frans de Waal, "Conformity to Cultural Norms of Tool Use in Chimpanzees," *Nature* 437 (September 29, 2005): 1-3.

[2]Bennett G. Galef, "Animal Traditions: Experimental Evidence of Learning by Imitation in an Unlikely Animal," *Current Biology: Dispatches* 20 (13).

[3]Francisco J. Ayala, "The Difference of Being Human: Morality," *Proceedings of the National Academy of Sciences* 107 (May 11, 2010): 9015-22.

[4]Steven Pinker, in "The Moral Instinct," *The New York Times Magazine*, January 13, 2008.

[5]Ayala, "The Difference of Being Human," p. 9016.

[6]Ibid., p. 9019, italics mine.

[7]Ibid., p. 9020.

[8]Patricia S. Churchland, *Braintrust: What Neuroscience Tells Us About Morality* (Princeton, NJ: Princeton University Press, 2011).

[9]Adina L. Roskies, "The Origins of Morality," *Nature* 472 (April 14, 2011): 166.

[10]"Does Moral Action Depend on Reasoning?" *Templeton Report*, May 26, 2010, pp. 1-52 <http://www.templeton.org/reason/>.

[11]Michael Gazzaniga, "Does Moral Action Depend on Reasoning? Not Really," *Templeton Report*, pp. 4-5.

[12]Ibid., p. 7, italics mine.

[13]Antonio Damasio, "Does Moral Action Depend on Reasoning? Yes and No," *Templeton Report*, p. 46.

[14]Jonah Lehrer, "Does Moral Action Depend on Reasoning? Not So Much," *Templeton Report*, p. 39.

[15]Ibid., p. 40.

[16]Ibid., italics mine.

11 What Is the Difference Between Altruism, Altruistic Love and Agape?

[1]A. Whiten, "Theory of Mind," in *Encyclopedia of Cognitive Science*, ed. L. Nadel, vol. 4 (London: Nature Publishing Group, 2005), p. 378.

[2]Giacomo Rizzolatti, Luciano Fadigo, Vittorio Gallese and Leonardo Fogassi, "Premotor Cortex and the Recognition of Motor Actions," *Cognitive Brain Research* 3 (1996): 131-41.

[3]Frans de Waal, *Good Natured: The Origin of Right and Wrong in Humans and Other Animals* (Cambridge, Mass.: Harvard, 1997), p. 209, italics mine.

[4]Ibid., p. 218.

[5]Martin A. Nowak with Roger Highfield, *Super Cooperators: Altruism, Evolution, and Why We Need Each Other to Succeed* (New York: Free Press, 2011).

[6]Ibid., p. 275.

[7]Lloyd Morgan, in *Oxford Companion to the Mind*, ed. R. L. Gregory (Oxford: Oxford University Press, 1987), p. 496.

[8]De Waal, *Good Natured,* p. 64.

[9]David G. Myers, *Intuition: Its Powers and Perils* (New Haven, Conn.: Yale University Press, 2002).

[10]Joan B. Silk and Bailey R. House, "Evolutionary Foundations of Human Prosocial Sentiments," Proceedings of the National Academy of Sciences 108 (June 28, 2011): 10910-17.

[11]Charles Taylor, *Sources of the Self: The Making of Modern Identity* (Cambridge, Mass.: Harvard University Press, 1989).

[12]Holmes Rolston III, "Kenosis and Nature," in *The Work of Love: Creation as Kenosis*, ed. John Polkinghorne (Grand Rapids: Eerdmans, 2001).

[13]Thomas Aquinas, *Summa Theologica.*

[14]Michael McCullough, in *Handbook of Religion and Health*, ed. Harold G. Koenig (Oxford: Oxford University Press, 2001).

[15]T. J. Bouchard Jr., D. T. Lykken, M. McGue, N. L. Segal and A. Tellegen, "Source of Human Psychological Differences: the Minnesota Study of Twins Reared Apart," *Science* 250 (1990): 223-28.

[16]Lindon Eaves, "Genetic and Social Influences on Religion and Values," in *From Cells to Souls—and Beyond: Changing Portraits of Human Nature*, ed. Malcolm Jeeves (Grand Rapids: Eerdmans, 2004), 102-22.

[17]Ibid.

[18]Ibid.

[19]Ibid.

12 Does Language Uniquely Define Us as Humans?

[1]S. Savage-Rumbaugh and K. McDonald, "Deception and Social Manipulation in Symbol-Using Apes," in *Machiavellian Intelligence: Social Expertise and the Evolution of Intellect in Monkeys, Apes and Humans*, ed. R. W. Byrne and A. Whitten (Oxford: Clarendon Press, 1988), p. 224-37.

[2]Personal email from Klaus Zuberbuhler, Oct. 19, 2012.

[3]Ibid.

[4]David Weatherall, chair, "The Use of Non-human Primates in Research," Report for the Academy of Medical Sciences, December 2006.

[5]Ibid., p. 59, italics mine.

[6]Ibid., p. 62.

[7]Ibid., pp. 63-64.

13 Does My Brain Have a "God Spot"?

[1]Carol R. Albright and James B. Ashbrook, *Where God Lives in the Human Brain* (Naperville, Ill.: Sourcebooks, 2001).

[2]Mary Ann Shaffer and Annie Barrows, *The Guernsey Literary and Potato Peel Pie Society* (New York: Random House, 2008), p. 227.

[3]Austin Farrer, *Saving Belief* (London: Hodder and Stoughton, 1964), p. 12.

[4]Michael A. Persinger, "Religious and Mystical Experiences as Artifacts of Temporal Lobe Function: A General Hypothesis," *Perceptual and Motor Skills* 57 (1983): 1255-62; Persinger, *Neuropsychological Bases of God Beliefs* (New York: Greenwood Press, 1987).

[5]Kevin S. Seybold, "God and the Brain: Neuroscience Looks at Religion," *Journal of Psychology and Christianity* 24 (2005): 122-29.

[6]J. L. Saver and J. Rabin, "The Neural Substrates of Religious Experience," *The Journal of Neuropsychology and Clinical Neurosciences* 9, no. 3 (1997): 498-510.

[7]Alexander A. Fingelkurts and Andrew A. Fingelkurts, "Is Our Brain Hardwired to Produce God, or Is Our Brain Hardwired to Perceive God? A Systematic Review on the Role of the Brain in Mediating Religious Experience," *Cognitive Processing* 10 (2009): 293-326.

[8]Ibid., p. 301.

[9]Ibid.

[10]Ibid.

[11]Ibid., p. 307.

[12]Ibid., p. 316.

[13]Andrew Newberg and Mark R. Waldman, *How God Changes Your Brain: Breakthrough Findings from a Leading Neuroscientist* (New York: Ballantine Books, 2009), p. 101.

[14]Miroslav Volf, *Free of Charge: Giving and Forgiving in a Culture Stripped of Grace* (Grand Rapids: Zondervan, 2005), p. 236.

[15]Mark S. George et al., "Daily Left Prefrontal Transcranial Magnetic Stimulation Therapy for Major Depressive Disorder: A Sham-Controlled Randomized Trial," *Archives of General Psychiatry* 67 (May 2010): 507-16.

[16]Isaak Walton and Charles Cotton, *The Complete Angler* (1676; repr. Oxford: Oxford University Press, 2009), p. 379.

[17]Diarmaid MacCulloch, *Christianity: The First Three Thousand Years* (New York: Penguin, 2009), p. 11.

14 Does God Guide and Direct Us?

[1]Antonio Damasio, *Descartes' Error: Emotion, Reason and the Human Brain* (New York: Putnam, 1994).

[2]Peter Enns, *The Evolution of Adam: What the Bible Does and Doesn't Say About Human Origins* (Grand Rapids: Brazos Press, 2012), p. 145.

[3]Ibid., p. 148.

[4]David G. Myers and Malcolm A. Jeeves, *Psychology Through the Eyes of Faith* (San Francisco:

HarperCollins, 2002), pp. 191-92.

15 Does Neuropsychology Have Anything to Offer Psychotherapy and Counseling?

[1]Eric L. Johnson, ed., *Psychology and Christianity: Five Views,* 2nd ed. (Downers Grove, Ill.: InterVarsity Press, 2010).

[2]Robyn M. Dawes, *House of Cards: Psychology and Psychotherapy Built on Myth* (New York: Free Press, 1994), p. 250.

[3]Paul R. Gross and Norman Levitt, *Higher Superstition: The Academic Left and its Quarrels with Science* (Baltimore: Johns Hopkins University Press, 1994), p. 234.

[4]Virginia Todd Holeman, "The Neuroscience of Christian Counseling," in *What About the Soul?* ed. Joel B. Green (Nashville: Abingdon, 2004), p. 152.

[5]Ibid., p. 155.

[6]M. J. Kempton et al., "Structural Neuroimaging Studies in Major Depressive Disorder," *Archives of General Psychiatry* 68 (2011): 675-90.

16 Are Religious Beliefs the Twenty-First-Century Opium of the People? *What About Placebo Effects?*

[1]David M. Myers, "Emotions, Stress and Health," in *Psychology,* 9th ed. (New York: Worth Publishers, 2010), pp. 497-602.

[2]Mario Beauregard, "Mind Does Really Matter: Evidence from Neuroimaging Studies of Emotional Self-Regulation, Psychotherapy, and Placebo Effect," *Progress in Neurobiology* 81 (2007): 232.

[3]Ted Kaptchuk et al., "No-Trickery Placebo," in *The Psychologist* 24 (February 2011): 88-89.

[4]Falk Eippert, J. Finsterbusch, W. Binsel and C. Buchel, "Direct Evidence for Spinal Cord Involvement in Placebo Analgesia," *Science* 326 (October 16, 2009): 404.

[5]Peter McNaughton, "Gene That Controls Chronic Pain Identified," *University of Cambridge Research News,* September 12, 2011 <http://www.cam.ac.uk/research/news/gene-that-controls-chronic-pain-identified/>.

17 What About Spirituality? *Is It a Separate "Religious" Part of Me?*

[1]Barbara Sahakian, "Test Could Detect Alzheimer's Disease Earlier," *University of Cambridge Research News,* May 16, 2011 <http://www.cam.ac.uk/research/news/test-could-detect-alzheimer%E2%80%99s-disease-earlier-than-previously-possible/>.

[2]N. T. Wright, *Surprised by Hope: Rethinking Heaven, the Resurrection, and the Mission of the Church* (London: SPCK, 2007), pp. 283-302.

[3]Glenn Weaver, "Embodied Spirituality: Experiences of Identity and Spiritual Suffering Among Persons with Alzheimer's Dementia," in *From Cells to Souls—and Beyond: Changing Portraits of Human Nature,* ed. Malcolm Jeeves (Grand Rapids: Eerdmans, 2004), pp. 77-101.

[4]Fraser Watts, ed., *Spiritual Healing: Scientific and Religious Perspectives* (New York: Cambridge University Press, 2011), p. 1.

[5]Ibid., p. 11.

[6]David A. Snowdon, "Aging and Alzheimer's Disease: Lessons from the Nun Study," *The Gerontologist* 37, no. 2 (1999): 150-56.

[7]Robert Davis, *My Journey into Alzheimer's Disease* (Wheaton, Ill.: Tyndale, 1989), p. 53.

[8]Ibid., p. 115.

[9]Lewis B. Smedes, *My God and I: A Spiritual Memoir* (Grand Rapids: Eerdmans, 2003).

[10]Ibid., p. 133.

[11]Tom Wright, *Paul for Everyone: The Prison Letters—Ephesians, Philippians, Colossians and Philemon* (London: SPCK, 2002), p. 23, italics mine.

18 Can Science "Explain Away" Religion?

[1]Francis Crick, *The Astonishing Hypothesis* (London: Simon and Schuster, 1994), p. 3.

[2]Roger W. Sperry, "American Psychological Association," *Psychological Science Agenda* (September-October 1994): 10-13.

[3]Sigmund Freud, *The Future of an Illusion* (New York: Classic House Books, 2009); Freud, *Civilization and Its Discontents* (New York: Penguin, 2002).

[4]H. C. Rumke, *The Psychology of Unbelief* (London: Rockliff, 1952).

[5]Gordon W. Allport, *The Individual and His Religion: A Psychological Interpretation* (London: Constable, 1951).

[6]Reijer Hooykaas, *Robert Boyle: A Study in Science and Christian Belief* (Lanham, Md.: University of America Press, 1997).

[7]Ibid.

[8]Athol Dickson, *The Gospel According to Moses* (Grand Rapids: Brazos, 2003), p. 21.

[9]Ibid., pp. 19, 24.

[10]Allport, *The Individual and His Religion,* p. 103.

[11]Ibid., p. vi.

[12]Frederick C. Bartlett, *Religion as Experience, Belief and Action* (Oxford: Oxford University Press, 1950).

[13]Justin L. Barrett, *Why Would Anyone Believe in God?* (Lanham, Md.: AltaMira Press, 2004).

[14]Justin L. Barrett, quoted in *The Psychologist* 24 (April 2011), p. 255.

[15]"Natural Born Believers: Why Religion Is Part of Human Nature," *New Scientist,* 2009.

[16]Dimitrios Kapogiannis et al., "Cognitive and Neural Foundations of Religious Belief," *Proceedings of the National Academy of Sciences* 106 (March 24, 2009): 4876-81.

[17]Elizabeth Culotta, "On the Origin of Religion," *Science* 326 (November 6, 2009): 784-87.

[18]John Stott, *The Radical Disciple: Some Neglected Aspects of Our Calling* (Downers Grove, Ill.: InterVarsity Press, 2010).

[19]C. Stephen Evans, *Preserving the Person: A Look at the Human Sciences* (Downers Grove, Ill.: InterVarsity Press, 1979).

[20]Mary van Leeuwen, *The Person in Psychology* (Grand Rapids: Eerdmans, 1985), p. 68.

[21]A. David Milner and Melvyn A. Goodale, *The Visual Brain in Action* (Oxford: Oxford University Press, 1995).

[22]Ibid., p. 42. For a brief update, see Mel Goodale and David Milner, "One Brain—Two Visual Systems," *The Psychologist* 19, no. 11 (November 2006): 660-63.

[23]Ibid., p. 66.

[24]Ibid., p. 204.

19 Where Next?

[1]Lisa Feldman Barrett, "The Future of Psychology: Connecting Mind to Brain," *Perspectives on Psychological Science* 4, no. 4 (2009): 326-39.

[2]Ibid., p. 326, italics mine.

[3]Ibid., p. 327.

[4]Ibid., p. 335.

[5]Ibid., p. 328, italics mine.

[6]Eleanor Maguire, in Greg Miller, "How Are Memories Retrieved?" *Science* 338, no. 1603 (October 5, 2012): 31.

[7]Ibid.

[8]Daniel Geschwind, in Greg Miller, "Why Is Mental Illness So Hard to Treat?" *Science* 338, no. 1603 (October 5, 2012): 33.

[9]Richard W. Byrne and Andrew Whiten, eds., *Machiavellian Intelligence: Social Expertise and the Evolution of Intellect in Monkeys, Apes, and Humans* (Oxford: Oxford University Press, 1989).

[10]R. I. M. Dunbar and Susanne Shultz, "Review: Evolution in the Social Brain," *Science* 317, no. 5843 (September 7, 2007): 1344-47.

[11]Francesca Happé, "When Will We Understand Autism Spectrum Disorders?" Rosalind Franklin Award Lecture, Royal Society of London, October 26, 2011. Reported in *The Psychologist* 24 (December 2011): 884-85.

[12]David Buss, "How Can Evolutionary Psychology Successfully Explain Personality and Individual Differences?" *Perspectives on Psychological Science* 4, no. 4 (2009): 359-66.

[13]Ibid., p. 360.

[14]Ibid.

[15]Ibid., p. 364.

[16]Ibid.

[17]J. M. Calcagno and A. Fuentes, "What Makes Us Human? Answers from Evolutionary Anthropology," *Evolutionary Anthropology* 21 (2012): 182-94.

[18]Steve Crabtree, "Religiosity Highest in World's Poorest Nations," Gallup World, August 31, 2010 <http://www.gallup.com/poll/142727/religiosity-highest-world-poorest-nations.aspx#1>.

[19]Justin L. Barrett and Matthew J. Jarvinen, "Evolutionary Byproducts and *Imago Dei*," in *The Emergence of Personhood: A Quantum Leap?* ed. Malcolm Jeeves (Grand Rapids: Eerdmans, forthcoming).

[20]Ibid.

[21]Ibid.

[22]Ibid.

[23]Ibid.

[24]Ibid.

[25]Ibid.

[26]Peter van Invagen, "Religious Belief as an Evolutionary Accident," in *The Believing Primate: Scientific, Philosophical, and Religious Reflections on the Origin of Religion*, ed. Michael Murray and Jeffrey Schloss (New York: Oxford University Press, 2010).

[27]Barrett and Jarvinen.

Name Index

Subject Index